Odiyal Kool, Kurakkan Puttu, an

RECIPES OF THE

JAFFNA TAMILS

Compiled by
Rani Thangarajah

Edited by
Nesa Eliezer

Orient Longman

ORIENT LONGMAN PRIVATE LIMITED

Registered Office
3-6-752 Himayatnagar, Hyderabad 500 029 (A.P.), India

Other Offices
Bangalore / Bhopal / Bhubaneshwar / Chennai
Ernakulam / Guwahati / Hyderabad / Jaipur / Kolkata
Lucknow / Mumbai / New Delhi / Patna

First published 2003

ISBN 81 250 2502 2

Typeset by
OSDATA, Hyderabad

Printed at
Baba Barkha Nath Printers
New Delhi

Published by
Orient Longman Private Limited
1/24 Asaf Ali Road
New Delhi 110 002

Contents

Introduction

The food traditions of a people express their attitudes to life. They are expressive not only of their geographical psyche but also of their beliefs about health and nutrition. They frequently summarise a people's views on interactive behaviour and etiquette.

In the case of the Tamils of the north and east of Sri Lanka, the regions referred to by Tamils as the Tamil Homelands or Tamil Eelam, the food traditions are characterised by a remarkable resourcefulness in their use of the locally available ingredients. In the Jaffna Peninsula (Yaalpaanam) the soil is harsh and arable only in pockets. But from this limited plenty the Tamils have created a cuisine that is so distinctive that it warrants closer interest than has been given it thus far. Tamils love their cuisine and wherever they go they relish the memories of it and try as far as possible to inculcate a love for it in their children.

I hope that this book recalls some of those memories, especially of the Jaffna Peninsula, in a meaningful way for the millions of Jaffna Tamils flung all over the globe. The mention of "Karupani" or "Susiyam" or "Pori Arisi Maa" brings a delighted twinkle to the eyes of Tamils in faraway lands. "Ah, yes, I remember my Amma used to. . . ." and off they go into warm, enchanting tales of a Jaffna childhood.

This book takes its spark from the warmth of that love for their land. The baths at Keerimalai, the tall, tufted palmyra trees swaying in cholai winds, the onion fields, the swollen kurakkan ears of grains on the sheaves, the oil monger grinding the goodness of the sesame seeds with his melancholy bull at the yoke . . . These memories are recounted in excited tones of beloved Tamil over hot meals of Odiyal Kool or Egg Hoppers in far-off lands.

The recipes have been lovingly compiled by Rani Thangarajah in Melbourne from friends and relatives both here and from Tamil Eelam. While every care has been taken to give a fairly comprehensive selection, this book cannot be exhaustive.

The book is intended mainly for Tamils who have settled overseas, from choice or necessity. I hope that it will provide them with a real link to their rich heritage.

As in all recipe books, the weights and measures and methods are those of the cooks. Every cook in the kitchen will make adjustments as her spirit and knowledge of taste lead her. Less chilli here, more salt there, a little more tamarind, leave out this, add that . . . what delights the trying of a recipe brings! I hope this book will prove to be no less exciting for lovers of Jaffna Tamil food everywhere.

Outside South and South East Asia, almost all the ingredients are available in most Asian groceries specialising in Sri Lankan and Indian produce in the major cities of Australia, Europe and the United States.

This book could not have been written without the help of the women of Melbourne who contributed the recipes from the storehouses of their mothers' and grandmothers' collections; I thank Dr Kanthi Kanavathipillay for help with translation from the Tamil. I also thank the family of the late S. Arumugam of Kuala Lumpur for permitting me to use excerpts from their family letters.

Nesa Eliezer

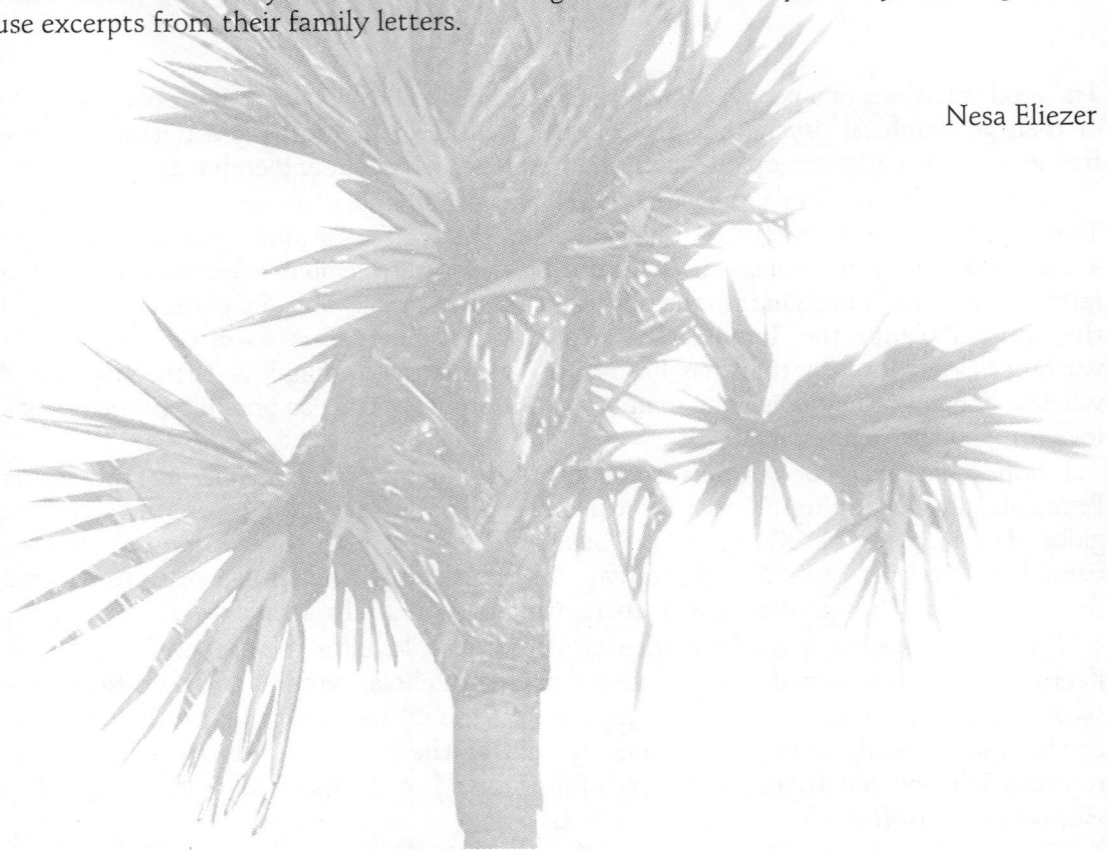

Breakfast Dishes

String Hoppers
Tomato Sothi
String Hopper Biryani
Rice Flour Puttu

Raagi Flour Puttu
Semolina Puttu
Aalanggai Puttu
Sugar Puttu

Black Gram Puttu
Spinach Puttu
Tapioca Puttu
Adai

Dosa
Ghee Thosai
Egg Thosai
Masala Dosa

Semolina Dosa
Wholemeal Flour Dosa
Idli
Coconut Milk Porridge
Upma

Vegetable Masala Upma
Hoppers
Sugar Hoppers
Egg Hoppers

String Hoppers

Idi-appam

2 cups roasted rice flour (white or red rice flour)
½ tsp salt
Boiling water as required

METHOD

1. Mix flour and salt. Add enough boiling water to form a paste that does not stick when touched.
2. Squeeze the paste through the ural to form string hoppers on to the steaming tray.
3. Steam till the string hoppers are not sticky to the touch.

Suggested accompaniments: Sothi, Coconut Chutney, Chicken or Mutton Curry.

Note: To make string hoppers, an 'ural' to form the hoppers is necessary. You will also need a steaming tray and a steamer.

Tomato Sothi

Thakkaali Sothi

2 tomatoes
3 cups water
3–4 green chillies, slit into two
5–6 (¼ tsp) fenugreek seeds
¼ tsp turmeric powder
½ cup thin coconut milk
½ tsp salt
½ cup thick coconut milk
1 tsp lime juice

METHOD

1. Boil tomatoes, water, green chillies, fenugreek seeds, turmeric, thin coconut milk and salt.
2. At first boil, add thick coconut milk. Allow it to come to a boil again. Remove from the stove.
3. Add lime juice, stir thoroughly, and serve hot.

Note: Traditionally, String Hoppers are accompanied by, amongst other dishes, a coconut milk stew called 'Sothi'. This can also be substituted with Tomato Sothi.

String Hopper 'Biryani'

Idi-appa Biryani

10–15 string hoppers
2 small potatoes, cut into small cubes
½ tsp chilli powder
½ tsp turmeric powder
½ tsp salt
2 tbsp oil
1 large onion, quartered and sliced
3 green chillies, sliced fine
1 sprig curry leaves
1 inch piece cinnamon stick
3 cloves
4 or 5 pieces cauliflower, broken into small flowerets
1 carrot, chopped fine
½ cup cabbage, chopped fine
1 leek, white part chopped fine
1 tsp finely chopped ginger
1 tsp coriander
1 tsp cumin seeds   } To be ground together
1 tsp black pepper } (or equivalent of powders to be mixed together)

Optional: *2 eggs, beaten lightly with pepper and salt to taste*

METHOD

1. Rub potato cubes with chilli powder, turmeric and ¼ teaspoon of the salt. Set aside for 10–15 minutes.
2. Break up the string hoppers into small pieces.
3. Heat oil in a pan. Fry potato cubes till almost cooked.

4. Add sliced onions. When transparent add green chillies, curry leaves, cinnamon and cloves. Saute till onions turn golden brown.
5. Add cauliflower, carrot, cabbage and leek. Add remaining salt and the chopped ginger. Cook till tender.
6. Add string hoppers. Mix thoroughly.
7. If egg is to be added, fry them in another pan.
8. Remove when cooked. Break up fried egg with a spatula. Add to string hoppers. Mix well.
9. Add ground aromatic spices. Mix well and remove from stove.
10. Add more salt if necessary.

Puttu

Puttu is a popular staple dish for both breakfast and dinner. It is traditionally steamed in a bamboo 'kulal'. This is a foot length of bamboo, about three inches in diameter, cut about an inch below a node. The lower part is 'turbaned' with a long piece of cotton cloth wound round it, while the rest of it is wound spirally with coir string. Resting on the node inside is a circular, perforated piece of coconut shell. The kulal rests on a vessel of boiling water and the puttu is steamed in it. It is really quite an attractive piece of kitchen equipment.

The other 'puttu steamer' is a 'neethu-petti' woven out of palm leaf. This is like a conical hat and the apex rests on the vessel of boiling water. Modern aluminum or stainless steel puttu steamers may not have the romance of these traditional ones but they do the job just as well.

Food processors are also used to mix puttu instead of the traditional 'hands on' method.

Rice Flour Puttu

Arisi-maa Puttu

4 cups roasted rice flour (white or red rice flour)
½ tsp salt
4 cups boiling water
1 cup freshly grated coconut

METHOD

1. In a large bowl, mix flour and salt with boiling water with a wooden spoon. As mixture cools mix flour with your hands to form a pebble-like texture.
2. In a kulal or puttu steamer, layer the flour mixture with a handful of grated coconut. Repeat the process till the kulal is almost filled. Finish with a layer of coconut.
3. Steam and serve hot.

Raagi Flour Puttu

Kurakkan Puttu

Kurakkan (Raagi or red millet) is grown commonly in the northern areas of Sri Lanka. Red millet flour is dark in colour and the puttu has a pleasing warm, dark tone as a result of this. Affectionately called "the black puttu", it is eaten with freshly scraped coconut and pieces of jaggery.

> 1 cup red millet (raagi, kurakkan) flour
> 1½ cups grated coconut
> Warm water as required
> Salt to taste

METHOD

1. Add salt to the warm water. Add water slowly to flour, stirring it with a wooden spoon to form a paste.
2. Using your hands, work mixture till it breaks into small round pieces.
3. Add grated coconut.
4. Steam in a puttu steamer—either the kulal or a neethu-petti.

Semolina Puttu

Ravai Puttu

> 2 cups semolina
> Salt to taste
> 1 cup water
> 1½ cups grated coconut

METHOD

1. Roast semolina slightly. Set aside to cool.
2. Add salt to semolina.
3. Add water and mix. Allow it to stand for half an hour.
4. Work the semolina with your fingers into small pebbles-like balls.
5. Add grated coconut.
6. Steam in the puttu steamer—either a kulal or a neethu-petti.

Aalanggai Puttu

Though called a puttu, this is also a sweet snack. It takes its name from its shape—like the fruit of the 'Aalai' (banyan) tree.

1 cup roasted rice flour (white or red rice flour)
¼ tsp salt
2 cups thin coconut milk
¼ cup roasted black gram (urad dal) flour
½ cup jaggery pieces
1½ cups thin coconut milk } syrup

METHOD

1. Mix rice flour and salt in a bowl.
2. Boil coconut milk.
3. Pour into flour and stir till smooth.
4. When the mixture has cooled add black gram flour and mix well.
5. Form into small balls, about 2 cm in diameter.
6. Steam in neethu-petti or any steaming vessel.
7. Boil the jaggery pieces and coconut milk into a syrup.
8. Add to the puttu. Stir and serve.

Sugar Puttu

Seeni Puttu

1 cup roasted rice flour (white or red rice)
½ cup roasted split green gram (moong dal)
1½ cups water
1 cup coconut milk
½ tsp salt
½ cup grated coconut
2 tbsp ghee
½ tsp cardamom powder (pounded cardamom seeds)
1½ cups sugar

METHOD

1. Wash the green gram and cook in water. Do not overcook—it should be whole, not mushy.
2. Drain and grind fine.
3. Boil coconut milk and salt.
4. Place rice flour in a bowl. Add the boiling coconut milk and stir to a grainy texture.

5. Add the ground green gram and grated coconut. Mix well.
6. Steam till cooked.
7. Transfer to a serving bowl. Add ghee, cardamom powder and sugar immediately. Mix well.
8. Serve warm.

Black Gram Flour Puttu

Uluthammaa Puttu

2 cups roasted white rice flour
1 cup roasted black gram (urad dal) flour
1 tsp salt
2½ cups water
2 cups grated coconut

METHOD

1. Boil water with salt.
2. Add to rice flour and mix to form a grainy texture.
3. When cool, add black gram flour and mix.
4. Add the grated coconut and mix together.
5. Steam in a puttu steamer.

Spinach Puttu

Keera Puttu

1 cup red millet (raagi/kurakkan) flour
200 grams spinach, chopped fine
Cold water as required
2 green chillies, chopped fine
4 medium-sized onions, chopped fine
½ cup grated coconut
½ tsp salt

METHOD

1. Mix red millet flour and spinach.
2. Sprinkle water and mix to form pebble-like balls. Sprinkle more water if required.

3. Add remaining ingredients and mix together. Ensure that the mixture retains its pebble-like consistency.
4. Steam in a puttu steamer.

Tapioca Puttu

Maravalli Puttu

1 cup tapioca flour, slightly roasted
1 cup grated coconut
3–4 green chillies, chopped
1 medium-sized onion, chopped fine
½ tsp salt

METHOD

1. Mix together tapioca flour, grated coconut, green chillies, onions and salt. Sprinkle water as you mix with your fingers, forming a grainy texture.
2. Steam in a puttu steamer.

Adai

½ cup split black gram (urad dal)
½ cup red gram (tuar dal)
½ cup chickpeas
1 cup grated coconut
2 cups parboiled rice
1 tsp salt
6 green chillies, chopped
10 dried red chillies, broken into small pieces
1 sprig curry leaves
A small piece of asafoetida soaked in a little warm water
(or ¼ tsp powdered asafoetida)
1 tbsp ghee or gingelly oil

METHOD

1. Soak black gram, red gram and chickpeas for at least 3–4 hours.
2. Grind all three together.
3. Add coconut and grind again.
4. Add the remaining ingredients except ghee/oil. Mix well.

5. Form small balls, the size of limes or ping-pong balls, and place on small squares of greaseproof paper or on an oiled piece of banana leaf. Press to form a little flat cake.
6. Heat a skillet or heavy non-stick pan, greased with a little oil.
7. Cook the 'pancakes' one at a time, perforating each with the edge of the cooking spatula to cook thoroughly. Turn over. Dribble a few drops of ghee/oil and turn over once more.
8. Remove and serve warm.

Dosa

Thosai

In India, this thin pancake made of rice and black gram flour is referred to as dosa. 'Thosai' is the Jaffna Tamil vernacular for it. It is commonly a breakfast dish but is often eaten as part of an evening meal as well. While gingelly oil is traditionally used to coat the skillet to fry the thosai, ghee is also used, though frowned upon by nutrition-conscious cooks.

> ½ cup parboiled rice (white)
> ½ cup long grain rice
> 1 cup black gram (urad dal), split and skinned
> 1 tsp fenugreek seeds
> 1 tsp salt

METHOD

1. Mix the two types of rice together and soak for at least 4 hours.
2. Soak black gram and fenugreek seeds, for at least 4 hours.
3. Grind all together till fine.
4. Allow to ferment overnight (or over a heater in cool temperatures).
5. Add salt. Stir thoroughly. Add water as required to make consistency right for frying on a skillet.
6. Heat a skillet or a non-stick pan. Grease with the gingelly oil or ghee.
7. Use a ladle to pour mixture onto the heated skillet or pan and spread with the ladle to form a circular pancake.
8. When bubbles form, flip it on to the other side to cook the thosai evenly.
9. Remove and serve hot.
10. Grease pan lightly again before making the next thosai.

VARIATIONS

Ghee Thosai: *After the thosai has been spread on the skillet, dribble ghee round the edges and a little all over the thosai, before turning it over. This forms a crisper, richer Ghee Thosai (called a "Ghee Murugal").*

Egg Thosai: *An egg can be broken on to the thosai directly. Allow to firm and flip half the thosai on to the other half (omelette style).*

Masala Dosa

Masala Thosai

Rice flour dosa mixture (as above)
Spicy dry potato curry:
4 potatoes, boiled, peeled and cubed
1 dessertspoon oil
¼ tsp fenugreek seeds
1 medium-sized onion, chopped
6–8 curry leaves cut fine
1 green chilli, chopped
1 dessertspoon curry powder*
½ tsp salt
¼ cup water

A combination of chilli powder, coriander powder, cumin seed powder and turmeric. Can be bought in most groceries.

Method

1. Heat oil in a pan. Add fenugreek seeds.
2. As soon as they turn golden add the chopped onion, curry leaves and green chilli. Cook till soft.
3. Add cubed potatoes, curry powder and salt.
4. Add water and mix thoroughly. Cook for about two minutes, turning constantly to prevent burning.
5. Remove and allow to cool a little.
6. Heat a skillet and make a thosai. When one side is cooked, place 2 dessertspoons of potato curry across the centre of the thosai. Fold the two sides of the thosai over the curry along the center.
7. Dish on to a plate and serve hot.

Semolina Dosa

Ravai Thosai

1 cup long grain rice, soaked and ground fine
1 cup plain flour (wheat)
1 cup semolina
2 cups buttermilk or
   2 cups thin coconut milk (1cup water mixed with 1 cup thick coconut milk)
1 tsp salt
2 tsp oil
½ tsp mustard seeds
½ tsp chopped ginger
6–8 curry leaves, chopped fine
5 green chillies, sliced fine
1 onion, chopped

METHOD

1. Mix ground rice, plain flour and semolina.
2. Add buttermilk (or coconut milk) and salt.
3. Leave to ferment for about an hour.
4. Heat oil and temper mustard seeds, ginger and curry leaves.
5. Add to the batter.
6. Add chopped green chillies and onion and water if necessary. The mixture should be thin enough to form a light pancake.
7. Heat a skillet. Stir the batter and make the thosai on the heated skillet.
8. When cooked fold in two and remove from skillet.

Wholemeal Flour Dosa

Aatamaa Thosai

2 cups wholemeal flour (aata/wheat flour) or 2 cups plain flour
¼ tsp baking powder
½ tsp salt
2½ cups water

METHOD

1. Mix all ingredients together. Leave to ferment for about half an hour.
2. Make the thosai on a greased, heated griddle. Perforate lightly with the edge of the spoon.
3. Dribble a little ghee on the thosai. Flip over to cook on the other side.
4. Remove when well cooked.

Idli

Ittali

> 2 cups parboiled rice
> ½ cup split black gram (urad dal)
> ½ tsp salt

METHOD

1. Soak rice and black gram separately for 4–6 hours.
2. Drain. Grind (fine) rice and black gram separately.
3. Mix the two and add salt. Allow to ferment for 12 hours.
4. Grease the idli mould with a little oil. Pour a small ladleful into each mould and steam for about 12–15 minutes.
5. Remove from moulds onto a dish. Serve hot.
6. Re-grease the mould and steam the next batch of idlis.

Coconut Milk Porridge

Thenggai Paal Kanchi

> 2 cups red rice (unroasted)
> 2 dessertspoons roasted split green gram (moong dal)
> 1 cup coconut milk
> ½ tsp salt
> 8 cups water

METHOD

1. Boil water. Add the rice and green gram.
2. When rice is very soft, add coconut milk and salt.
3. Serve with coconut chutney.

Upma

Uppumaa

> 1 cup semolina, roasted well
> 2 cups water
> 2 dessertspoons ghee or gingelly oil
> 1 dried red chilli, broken into pieces

1 tsp mustard seeds
2 tsp split black gram (urad dal)
1 medium onion, chopped
3 green chillies, sliced fine
5–8 curry leaves, cut fine
1 tsp salt
1 tiny piece asofoetida, dissolved, or ¼ tsp powdered asafoetida (optional)

METHOD

1. Heat oil in a pan. Add dried chilli pieces, mustard seeds and split black gram.
2. Add chopped onion, green chillies and curry leaves. Stir for a minute or so until onion softens.
3. Add water, salt and asafoetida. Bring to boil.
4. Add semolina, a little at a time, stirring constantly so as not to form lumps.
5. Cook, turning mixture over constantly to prevent burning.
6. Remove and transfer to a serving dish. Press and cover for about 5 minutes. Lift the lid and give the uppumaa a stir and serve warm.
7. Sometimes the uppumaa can be pressed into small bowls and overturned onto a plate to form little mounds before serving.

Optional: 2 teaspoons of lime/lemon juice can be added to the uppumaa to give it a delicious tang.

Vegetable Masala Upma

Marakari Uppumaa

1 cup roasted semolina
2 cups light coconut milk
2 tsp tamarind pulp
1 tsp salt
3 dessertspoons oil
1 tsp mustard seeds
1 tsp split black gram (urad dal)
1 tsp Bengal gram (channa dal)
1 cup young eggplant (brinjal), chopped fine
¼ cup carrots chopped fine
¼ cup chopped leek (optional)
¼ cup potatoes chopped small
4–6 green chillies, chopped fine
1 medium-sized onion, chopped fine
½ tsp finely chopped ginger

6–8 curry leaves, chopped fine
A pinch turmeric powder
½ tsp chilli powder
A tiny piece asafoetida soaked in a tsp warm water or
   ¼ tsp powdered asafoetida
1 dessertspoon ghee

METHOD

1. Mix together coconut milk, tamarind pulp and salt. Set aside.
2. Heat oil in a pan. Sauté mustard seeds, split black gram and Bengal gram.
3. Add all the vegetables, green chillies, chopped onion, ginger, curry leaves, turmeric and chilli. Turn constantly and cook till aroma rises.
4. Add coconut milk mixture and asafoetida. Bring to boil.
5. Add semolina, a little at a time, stirring constantly to prevent it from forming lumps, till cooked.
6. Remove from the stove and add ghee. Mix well.
7. Transfer to a serving dish and cover for a few minutes.
8. Remove the lid and stir before serving warm.

Hoppers

Appam

2 cups white rice flour
1 tsp dry yeast
1 tsp sugar
1 cup water
1 cup coconut milk
¼ tsp baking powder
½ tsp salt

METHOD

1. Add yeast and sugar to half cup water. Leave for 10 minutes or so, till it froths.
2. Place rice flour in a bowl. Make a well in the centre and pour yeast mixture in. Stir to form a paste. Add remaining water if necessary.
3. Cover and leave to ferment for at least 12 hours.
4. Set aside 4 tablespoons of coconut milk, adding the rest to the dough.
5. Add baking powder and salt. Mix thoroughly and set aside for half an hour.
6. Heat the little 'hopper pan' and grease it by brushing the surface with a piece of cloth dipped in oil. Pour 2 tablespoons of batter and, lifting the pan off the stove, rotate so that the batter coats the sides. Cook over medium flame.

7. Cover with a lid and cook for about 3–4 minutes. Lift the lid. The edges should have turned brown.
8. Remove lid. (Some of the coconut milk set aside earlier can be spooned into the centre of the hopper if a creamier centre is desired. Allow to cook.) Slide hopper out of pan with a wooden spatula.
9. The plain hoppers may be eaten with the remaining coconut milk and coconut chutney.

VARIATION:

Sugar (Seeni) Hoppers: *A little jaggery or sugar may be added to the centre at step 7.*

Egg Hoppers: *Pour 2 tablespoons of batter in the hopper pan. Tilt and rotate pan till batter coats the sides. Break an egg into the centre, taking care not to break the yolk. Cover with lid, until cooked. Slide the hopper out of the pan with a wooden spatula. Serve hot.*

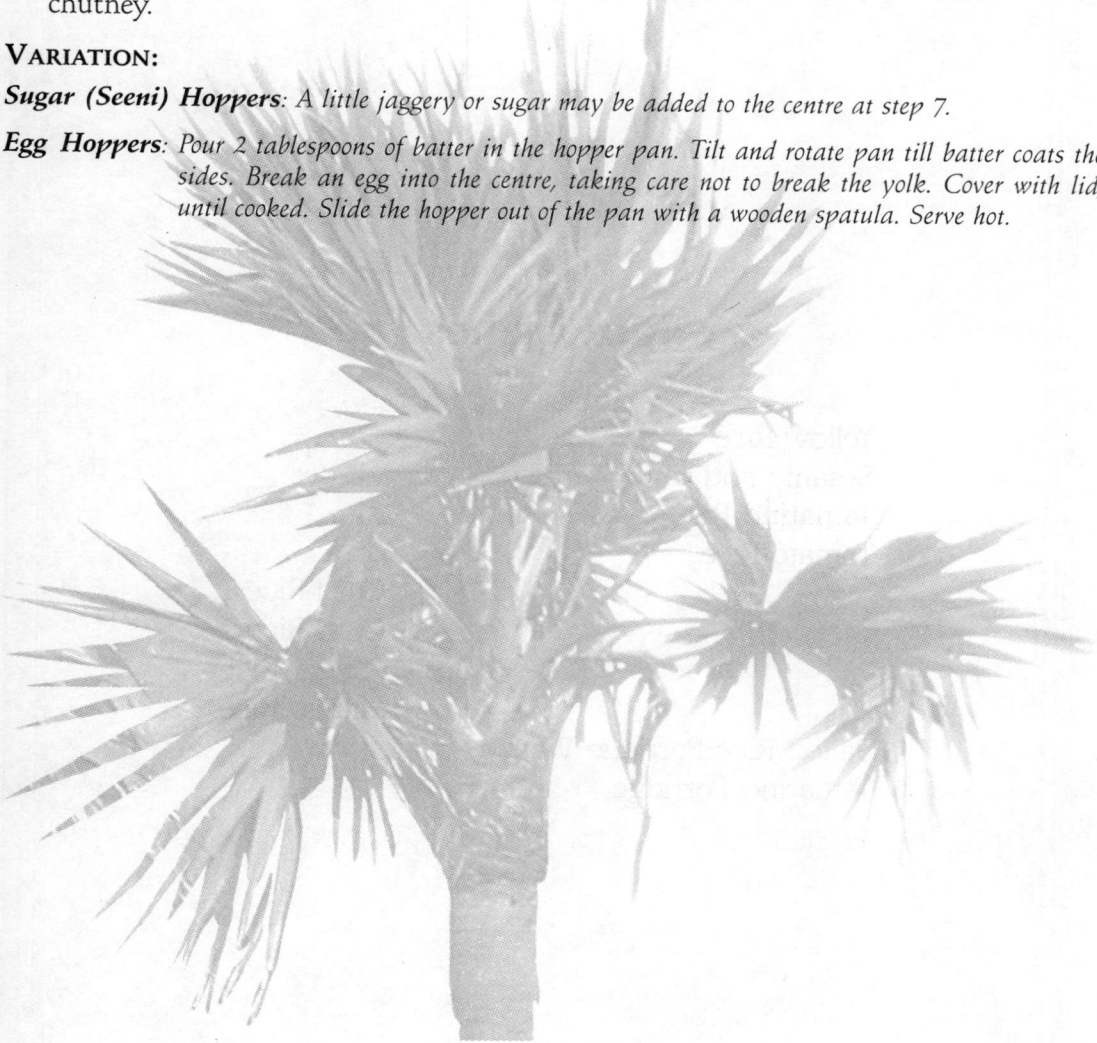

Rice Dishes

Yellow Rice
Sesame and Coconut Rice
Tamarind Rice
Tomato Rice

Curd Rice 1
Curd Rice 2
Brown Sugar Rice
Mango Rice

Salted Rice Porridge Water
Tamarind Porridge

Yellow Rice

Manchal Choru

4 cups washed rice
6 cardamom pods
6 cloves
1-inch piece cinnamon stick
12 black peppercorns (milagu), whole
A pocket handkerchief-sized fine cotton or muslin cloth
1 dessertspoon ghee
6 cloves garlic
1 cup chopped onion
1 sprig curry leaves
1 rampe (pandanus or screwpine) leaf
1½ cups coconut milk
A few strands saffron soaked for few minutes in a tablespoon of warm water
   (or ½ tsp turmeric powder)
1tsp salt
1½ cups water

METHOD

1. Finely pound (or dry grind) cardamom, cloves, cinnamon and peppercorn. Tie in a bundle in the cloth.
2. Heat ghee in pan on a low flame. Add garlic, chopped onion, curry leaves and rampe leaf.
3. Fry for about two minutes and then add the coconut milk, soaked saffron (or turmeric) and salt.
3. Add water and bring to boil.
4. Add the washed rice and the bundle of ground spices.
5. Stir and simmer uncovered for 15 minutes (until the liquid is absorbed).
6. Remove from stove and allow to stand for 5 minutes. Remove spice bundle before serving.

Sesame and Coconut Rice

Ellu Thenggai Saatham

1 cup rice
2 tbsp split black gram (urad dal)
¼ cup sesame seeds (white)
1 cup dessicated coconut
1 tbsp gingelly oil
8 dried red chillies
1 sprig curry leaves
1 tbsp ghee
1 tbsp mustard seeds
25 raw cashew nuts, chopped
7 green chillies, diced

METHOD

1. Cook rice and allow to cool.
2. In a little water, soak 1 tablespoon black gram for ½ an hour.
3. In a dry pan, roast sesame seeds till golden and set aside.
4. Heat gingelly oil and fry remaining (1 tablespoon) black gram, half the dried chillies and curry leaves for about two minutes.
5. Remove from stove, add the roasted sesame seeds and grind to a fine paste.
6. Drain black gram.
7. Heat ghee in a pan. When hot, fry mustard seeds, remaining dried chillies, chopped cashew nuts, green chillies and the drained black gram for about two minutes.
8. Add coconut and fry with tempered ingredients till golden.
9. Remove from stove. Mix in the ground paste.
10. Fold in the rice, spoon by spoon, till mixed well.

Tamarind Rice

Puli Choru or Puli Saatham

1 cup rice
1 tbsp tamarind paste
½ tsp turmeric powder
1 tsp salt
4 tbsp ghee or gingelly oil

1 tsp mustard seeds
1 tsp fennel seeds
1 tbsp black gram (urad dal)
5 dried red chillies, broken into pieces
1 sprig curry leaves
1 tbsp Bengal gram (channa dal) or split peas
½ cup water

METHOD

1. Cook rice and allow to cool.
2. Mix tamarind paste, turmeric and salt together and set aside.
3. Heat ghee in a pan and fry mustard seeds, fennel seeds, black gram, dried chillies, curry leaves, and Bengal gram for about two minutes.
4. Add water and tamarind paste and bring to boil. Reduce heat to a low flame.
5. Fold in the rice, a spoon at a time and mix well. Serve hot or cold.

"The train sped on, taking me from the ones I loved to an unknown world of the city. I could hear, with every roll of the steel wheels against the hard, unforgiving iron rails, the sounds of home getting farther. The fields, the trees, the egrets sitting on patient cows, all blurred into one in a teary world.

I sat back against the seat. I resigned myself to this hard journey, to a life I only dimly comprehended to be 'my future'. Next to me lay the chothupetti [tiffin carrier, a container commonly seen as a set of three, stacked one above the other and then slipped on to a contraption that linked all three, so that they could be carried as one], tied in a bundle with a soft well-worn square cloth cut from some discarded dress or skirt of my sister's. I untied it, and lifted the lid of the chothupetti. Ahhh! The smell, the scent, the joy! Puli saatham! The tamarind rice my mother was famed for!

I ate it slowly, savouring each mouthful through tears. I could almost smell Amma in the rich, sour-hot rice. I had eaten Puli saatham many times on former outings to Keerimalai or Kathirgamam. But none of them tasted like this one: this was ambrosia. It was home.

S. Arumugam: "Letters from Jaffna"

Tomato Rice

Thakkaali Saatham

2 cups long grain rice
500 gm ripe tomatoes
1 tsp salt
6 tbsp ghee or gingelly oil
1 medium-sized onion, diced
6 green chillies, chopped
1 tsp mustard seeds
6 garlic cloves, crushed
5 dried red chillies, broken into pieces
1 sprig curry leaves
¼ tsp cumin seed powder
¼ tsp ground white pepper
4 tsp lime or lemon juice

METHOD

1. Cook the rice and set aside.
2. Blanch the tomatoes.
3. Chop tomatoes into small pieces. Mash lightly and add salt.
4. Heat ghee or gingelly oil in a pan. Fry the onions, green chillies, mustard seeds, crushed garlic, dried chillies and curry leaves.
5. Add cumin powder and white pepper.
6. Add mashed tomato and lime/lemon juice.
7. Mix well and remove from stove.
8. Fold in rice, a spoon at a time, and mix well. Serve hot or cold.

Curd Rice 1

Thayir Saatham

2 cups rice (long grain or basmati)
2 cups curd (yoghurt)
1tsp salt
1 tsp mustard seeds
3 tbsp oil
1 tsp split black gram (urad dal)
8 dried red chillies, broken into pieces
6–8 curry leaves
½ tsp chopped ginger

METHOD

1. Cook the rice and set aside.
2. Mix curd and salt together.
3. Roast mustard seeds in a heated pan till they pop.
4. Add oil. When hot, fry black gram, dried chillies and curry leaves for a minute or so.
5. Add chopped ginger and fry all together.
6. Remove from the stove. Add to the curd mixture and mix well.
7. Place mixture in a large container and fold in rice, a spoon at a time, to mix well.
8. Serve warm or cold.

Curd Rice 2

Thayir Saatham

2 cups rice
1 cup curd (yogurt)
1½ tbsp ghee
2 green chillies, chopped fine
½ tsp mustard seeds
1 tbsp split black gram (urad dal)
6–8 curry leaves
2 dried red chillies, chopped fine
1 tbsp grated ginger
½ tsp salt

METHOD

1. Cook the rice and set aside.
2. Heat ghee in a pan and fry green chillies, mustard seeds, black gram, curry leaves, dried chillies and ginger. Remove from the stove.
3. Mix the curd and salt. Add to the rice and mix well.

Brown Sugar Rice

Chakkarai Saatham (Chakkarai Pukkai)

This dish is often cooked on ceremonious or auspicious occasions, and sometimes when people fast. It is especially significant on Thaipongal, the first day of the month of Thai, to celebrate the harvest and offer homage to the sun.

1 cup long grain rice
½ cup split green gram (moong dal), roasted

2½–3 cups water
1 cup coconut milk
1 cup brown sugar (or jaggery pieces)
2 dessertspoons ghee
2 tbsp cashew nuts, chopped
2 tbsp raisins
½ tsp cardamom seed powder (or crushed cardamom seeds)

METHOD

1. Soak rice for half an hour and drain.
2. Bring water to boil. Add rice and green gram.
3. When rice is cooked add coconut milk and brown sugar.
4. Remove from stove.
5. Heat ghee in a pan. Sauté cashew nuts and raisins. Turn off flame. Add cardamom powder. Remove and add to rice. Mix well.
6. Serve warm or cold.

"Amma lay the ulakkai [heavy staff used to pound rice in a wooden mortar or ural] on the clean sand in front of the house and drew a pattern of squares with rice flour. I watched as she bent in the dim light of dawn drawing the pattern of the kolam. How cleverly she drew a sun in the centre of the pattern. She stood up, faced the east, lifted her hands in silent prayer to the sun which was still on its way.

She continued to finish the drawing and then made a kind of stove with bricks in the centre of the kolam, in the middle of the sun she had drawn. Upon this the pongal pot would rest. She sang softly to herself, to the gods of her choice and set the pot upon the stove. She had tied a garland of mango leaves around the neck of the new earthen pot Father had bought.

The pongal of chakkarai pukkai had to be ready before the sun rose. All of us waited round while Father and Mother both sang hymns softly. It was a special day, all right. And we would have beautiful, gooey, sweet chakkarai pukkai for breakfast!

S. Arumugam: "Letters from Jaffna"

Mango Rice

Maamabala Saatham

2 cups long grain rice
4 cups water
1 tsp salt
4 cups mango pulp

½ cup sugar (more if required)

4 tsp ghee

1 tsp mustard seeds

2 dried red chillies, broken into pieces

1 sprig curry leaves

METHOD

1. Bring water to boil and cook the rice.
2. When cooked, add salt, mango pulp and sugar.
3. Cook on a low flame for a further 10 minutes. Remove.
4. Heat ghee in a pan and sauté mustard seeds, dried chillies and curry leaves.
5. Remove from stove and add to rice. Mix well before serving.

Salted Rice Porridge Water

Kanchi Thanni (Uppu Kanji)

Kanchi Thanni is prepared for invalids who have difficulty either swallowing or digesting whole food. It distils the nutrients from the grain to aid recovery.

500 grams long grain or 'red rice'

2 l water

6–8 cloves garlic

Thumb-sized piece of ginger, chopped fine

¼ tsp salt

METHOD

1. Boil rice in water with garlic, ginger and salt.
2. When rice is very soft, mash it with the back of a ladle.
3. Strain rice. The thick rice water can be served as is or can be diluted with a little warm water.

Tamarind Porridge

Puli Kanchi

½ cup parboiled rice

4 cups water

5 small onions or ½ large onion, chopped

10 cloves garlic

20 medium-sized prawns or 3 tbsp dried prawns

1 tsp chilli powder
a pinch, turmeric powder, mixed in ½ cup water
1 tbsp coriander
½ tsp pepper   ground together
½ tsp cumin seeds
1½ tsp tamarind pulp
4 tbsp coconut milk
a handful drumstick leaves
2 green chillies, chopped
Salt to taste

METHOD

1. Wash and cook rice in 2 cups of water.
2. When water begins to boil, add onions, garlic, prawns, chilli powder and turmeric water. Boil them together.
3. Once rice is cooked, add ground spices, tamarind pulp and add another 2 cups of water.
4. Add coconut milk, drumstick leaves, green chillies and salt to taste.
5. Allow to boil till it thickens.
6. Remove from stove.

Vegetarians: Omit prawns. Add cubed brinjal (aubergines), pieces of unripe bananas (green banana) and jackfruit seeds.

Puli kanchi has special connotations when the rains start:

"As the rains began to beat their tempo upon our roof, we gathered in Appa's rest room—always smelling of warm cheroot and coffee. Appa would lie on his easy-chair reading his Ananda Vikadan, while my brother, Rajadurai, would lounge on his worn leather chair gazing out of the window, watching the falls from the eaves edging the verandah. Just as I was about to stretch my hand out of the other window to reach for the rain, Amma came in.

"Puli kanchi!" she beamed. All action now. We moved to Appa's table as Amma laid the kottangachi (half coconut shells polished to become bowls) of puli kanchi out for us.

"Ah," said Appa, raising the delightful bowl to his lips, "The rain and puli kanchi!" He sounded like a god drinking ambrosia. We said nothing, as we allowed its warm, spicy, sour, hot comfort to warm our throats and move like a river down to our stomachs.

S. Arumugam: "Letters from Jaffna"

Pachadis and Chambals

Green Banana Flower Pachadi
Green Banana Pachadi
Green Banana Skin Pachadi
Hibiscus Flower and Yoghurt Pachadi

Ginger Pachadi
Tomato Pachadi
Bitter Gourd and Yoghurt Pachadi
Potato Pachadi
Mango and Yoghurt Pachadi

Cucumber and Yoghurt Pachadi
Cucumber and Coconut Milk Pachadi
Snake Gourd and Yoghurt Pachadi
Okra Pachadi
Jackfruit Pachadi
Indian Pennywort Leaves Pachadi

Indian Pennywort Chambal
Ginger Chambal
Coconut Chambal
Green Chilli Chambal

Sesame Chambal
Hot Coconut Chambal
Onion Chutney
Pumpkin Chutney
Tomato Chutney

Date and Tomato Chutney
Chutney Podi
Thosai Podi

Green Banana (Ash Plantain) Flower Pachadi

Vaalappu Pachadi

1   ash plantain flower (other types may be too bitter), chopped very fine
1½ cups   buttermilk (or 2 cups water with 2 tsp salt)
4 tbsp   oil
5   dried red chillies, broken into pieces
½ tsp (less than)   mustard seeds
6–8   curry leaves
5   green chillies, chopped fine
½ cup   coconut, grated
5 tbsp   coconut milk
3 medium-sized onions, chopped fine
4 tsp   lime /lemon juice

Method

1. Soak chopped ash plantain flower in buttermilk (or salt water) for at least ½ an hour. Drain and squeeze dry.
2. Heat oil. Fry dried chillies, mustard seeds and curry leaves.
3. Add ash plantain flower and green chillies. Toss together.
4. Add the grated coconut and coconut milk. Milk well.
5. Add chopped onions and lime/lemon juice and remove from stove.

Green Banana (Ash Plantain) Pachadi

Vaalakkaai Pachadi

4   raw ash plantains
½ cup   scraped coconut, ground coarse
5 tbsp   coconut milk

4 green chillies, chopped fine
1½ medium-sized (or 1 large) onions, chopped fine
1 sprig curry leaves, chopped fine
Salt to taste
4–5 tsp lime/lemon juice
1 dried red chilli, broken into small pieces ⎫
½ tsp mustard seeds ⎬ for seasoning
2 tsp oil or ghee ⎭

METHOD

1. Grill or roast whole bananas.
2. Skin when cool.
3. Mash the flesh of the bananas.
4. Add all the ingredients and mix well.
5. Heat oil or ghee. Add dried chilli and mustard seeds and fry till a few seeds pop.
6. Add to the banana pachadi and mix well before serving.

Green Banana (Ash Plantain) Skin Pachadi

Vaalakkaai Thol Pachadi

Skin of 2 ash plantains
½ cup water
Thumb-sized piece of ginger
¼ cup scraped (or dessicated) coconut
1 medium-sized onion, chopped fine
1 green chilli, chopped fine
2 tbsp coconut milk
1½ tsp lime/lemon juice
½ tsp salt
2 tsp oil or ghee ⎫
1 dried red chilli, broken into small pieces ⎪
1 sprig curry leaves ⎬ for seasoning
½ tsp mustard seeds ⎭

METHOD

1. Peel outer green skin of ash plantain. Chop fine.
2. Cook in water till half done.
3. Remove from water and grind coarsely with ginger and coconut.
4. Add chopped onions, green chilli, coconut milk, lime/lemon juice and salt.

5. Heat oil or ghee. Add dried chilli, curry leaves and mustard seeds.
6. Add to the pachadi and mix well.

Hibiscus Flower and Yoghurt Pachadi

Semparathappu-Thayir Pachadi

20–25 hibiscus (shoeflower) flowers, chopped fine
½ tsp ghee
½ cup coconut shreds (scraped coconut)
¾ dessertspoon thick yoghurt
½ tsp salt
1½ tsp lime/lemon juice
3 tsp oil
½ tsp mustard seeds
4 dried red chillies, broken into small pieces
6–8 curry leaves

METHOD
1. Heat ghee and sauté hibiscus flowers in it.
2. Mix together grated coconut, yoghurt, salt and lime/lemon juice.
3. Heat oil in pan and temper mustard seeds, dried chillies and curry leaves.
4. Add hibiscus flowers. Fold in well and remove from stove.
5. Fold into yoghurt mixture.

Ginger Pachadi

Inji Pachadi

5 cm piece of fresh ginger
1 cup scraped (or dessicated) coconut
¾ tsp salt
6–8 curry leaves, chopped fine
1 onion, chopped fine
6 green chillies, chopped fine
2 tsp lime/lemon juice
2 tsp oil or ghee
1 dried red chilli, broken into small pieces } *for seasoning*
½ tsp mustard seeds

METHOD

1. Scrape and chop ginger coarsely. Grind fine. (Alternatively, grate ginger extremely fine.)
2. Grind coconut coarsely. Add to ground ginger.
3. Add salt, curry leaves, onion, green chillies and lime/lemon juice.
4. Mix well.
5. Heat oil or ghee. Add dried chilli and mustard seeds and stir till a few seeds pop.
6. Add to the ginger pachadi mixture. Mix well.

Tomato Pachadi

Thakkaali Pachadi

4 tomatoes, chopped into small pieces
1 dessertspoon oil
1 tsp mustard seeds
¼ tsp fenugreek seeds
1 medium-sized onion, chopped fine
2 green chillies, chopped fine
1 tsp grated fresh ginger
1 small sprig curry leaves, chopped fine
Salt to taste
½ cup yoghurt

METHOD

1. Heat oil in a pan. Fry mustard and fenugreek seeds.
2. Add onions and sauté till transparent.
3. Add green chillies, ginger and curry leaves. Sauté for a minute or so.
4. Add tomatoes and salt to taste. Cook till tomatoes are done but still reasonably firm.
5. Remove from stove. When slightly cool, add yoghurt and mix well.

Potato Pachadi

Urulakkilangu Pachadi

100 gm potatoes, boiled and skinned
6 green chillies, chopped fine
¼ cup coconut milk

¼ tsp salt
3 tsp lime/lemon
1 onion, chopped fine
2 tsp oil or ghee
1 dried red chilli, broken into small pieces
6–8 curry leaves, chopped fine   } for seasoning
½ tsp mustard seeds

METHOD

1. Mash potatoes. Add all ingredients and mix well.
2. Heat oil. Add dried chilli, curry leaves and mustard seeds and fry till a few seeds pop.
3. Add to potato mixture and fold in well.

Bitter Gourd and Yoghurt Pachadi

Paavakkaai Pachadi

1 bitter gourd, grated
2 cups coconut water or 2 cups water with 2 tsp salt
1 tbsp green mango, grated
4–5 tbsp grated coconut
6 tbsp yoghurt
3 green chillies, chopped fine
½ tsp salt
2 tsp oil or ghee
1 dried chilli, broken into small pieces
½ tsp mustard seeds   } for seasoning
6–8 curry leaves, chopped

METHOD

1. Soak grated bitter gourd in coconut water or salted water for about ½ an hour.
2. Drain and squeeze dry.
3. Add all other ingredients and mix well.
4. Heat oil. Fry dried red chillies, mustard seeds and curry leaves for a minute.
5. Add to the pachadi and mix well.

Mango and Yoghurt Pachadi

Maanggaai Pachadi

1 green mango, grated
1 medium-sized onion
½ tsp mustard seeds
6–8 curry leaves
5 tbsp grated coconut
3 green chillies, chopped fine
½ cup yoghurt
¼ tsp salt
2 tsp oil or ghee
1 dried red chilli, broken into small pieces ⎫ for seasoning
½ tsp mustard seeds ⎭

METHOD

1. Grind onion, mustard seeds and curry leaves, coarsely.
2. Put rest of the ingredients in a bowl. Add ground mixture.
3. Heat oil. Fry dried chillies and mustard seeds till a few seeds pop.
4. Add to the pachadi and mix well.

Cucumber and Yoghurt Pachadi

Kekkarikkai Thayir Pachadi

1 cucumber
½ cup yoghurt
½ tsp salt
1 tbsp grated coconut
2 green chillies, chopped fine
1 medium-sized onion (red Spanish onion or 5 small rose onions), chopped fine
5–7 curry leaves, chopped fine
1 tsp lime/lemon juice
1 tsp oil ⎫ for seasoning
½ tsp mustard seeds ⎭

METHOD

1. Cut both ends of the cucumber and remove any bitterness by rubbing each cut end over the cucumber. Wipe away the white sap with a kitchen towel.
2. Skin, cut in half and remove seeds.
3. Grate cucumber coarsely. Add salt and set aside for about ten minutes.

4. Press grated cucumber over a sieve to remove all liquid (or strain through a muslin cloth and squeeze out the liquid).
5. Grind grated coconut, not too fine.
6. Mix yoghurt, ground coconut, green chillies, chopped onion, curry leaves and lime/lemon juice.
7. Add the grated cucumber. Mix well and add more salt if necessary.
8. Heat oil in a pan. Splutter mustard seeds. Add to pachadi.

Cucumber and Coconut Milk Pachadi

Kekkarikkai Thenggaipaal Pachadi

1 cucumber
2 green chillies, chopped fine
3–4 rose onions or 1 medium-sized red onion, chopped fine
3 tbsp coconut milk
Salt to taste

METHOD

1. Cut both ends of the cucumber and remove any bitterness by rubbing each cut end over the cucumber. Wipe away the white sap with a kitchen towel.
2. Cut ends off to the point where seeds begin to show.
3. Skin. Score the sides with a fork.
4. Slice very fine circles.
5. Mix with the rest of the ingredients.

Snake Gourd and Yoghurt Pachadi

Pidalanggaai Pachadi

Snake gourd is grown on 'panthals' or stick canopies. The plant spreads itself and as the long, thin gourds appear, small stones are tied to their ends to make them grow straight.

1 young snake gourd
½ cup scraped coconut
¾ cup yoghurt
1 medium-sized onion, chopped fine

3 green chillies, chopped fine
6 curry leaves, chopped fine
2 tsp lime/lemon juice
2 tsp oil or ghee
1 dried red chilli, broken into small pieces } for seasoning
½ tsp mustard seeds

METHOD

1. Cut snake gourd into two. Cut down the middle of each half and remove seeds and white pulp. Scrape as much of the outer skin as possible.
2. Slice and steam the pieces. Do not over-steam. The pieces should be firm.
3. Remove. When cool, squeeze dry.
4. Grind coconut coarsely.
5. Add to snake gourd together with the rest of the ingredients.
6. Heat oil. Fry dried chilli and mustard seeds till they pop.
7. Add to pachadi and mix well before serving.

Okra (Ladies' Fingers) Pachadi

Vendikkaai Pachadi

500 grams okra, thinly sliced
2 tsp oil
1 tsp tamarind pulp
1 tsp cumin seed powder
1 tsp coriander powder
1 tsp chilli powder
Salt to taste
1 cup water

METHOD

1. Heat oil in a pan. Add the okra and sauté over medium heat until tender and soft.
2. Add tamarind pulp, cumin, coriander, chilli powder and salt.
3. Add water. Bring to a boil.
4. Stir and cook for 5 minutes. Serve warm.

Note: Okra should be washed whole and allowed to dry, or dried with a dishcloth before cutting to prevent the sticky fluid from oozing out.

Jackfruit Pachadi

Pilaakkaai Pachadi

500 grams young jackfruit, flesh and seeds chopped
½ tsp salt
½ cup water
1 cup grated coconut
2 green chillies, chopped fine
1 Bombay or 5 rose onions, chopped fine

METHOD

1. Add salt to the water.
2. Boil jackfruit in salted water till soft. Remove.
3. Add grated coconut, chopped green chillies and onions.
4. Mix well.

Indian Pennywort (Gotu Kola) Leaves Pachadi

Vallaarai Chambal

100 gm Indian Pennywort leaves
½ cup grated coconut
10 rose onions sliced or 1 large onion, chopped
6 green chillies, chopped
5–7 curry leaves, chopped fine
½ tsp salt
1 tbsp lime/lemon juice

METHOD

1. Wash the leaves and chop fine.
2. Mix together with grated coconut, onions, green chillies, curry leaves and salt.
3. Add lime/lemon juice. Mix well. Set aside for 15–20 minutes before serving.

Chambals (Sambals)

A 'chambal', or 'sambal', has connotations of being ground, usually with grated coconut. It is also referred to as an 'arayal', literally 'that which has been ground'. A chambal would be termed 'chutney' by most Indians.

The family grinding stone (the ammi) has an important place in the kitchen precincts, as many recipes in Tamil cuisine require grinding. It comprises a flat slab and an elliptical grinding stone on it that pulverises the ingredients to be ground. The granite stone is regularly treated by being pitted all over with a nail and hammer by the itinerant 'ammi-kuthukaaran'.

With the blenders and food processors of today, the ammi has been relegated to becoming almost a token presence in the Tamil kitchen. It makes its presence felt, however, in marriage ceremonies when it features in ritual as a symbol of the steadfast loyalty of a bride to her husband.

Indian Pennywort (Gotu Kola) Chambal

Vallaarai Chambal

2 cups Indian Pennywort leaves, cut small
2–3 tsp ghee
2 dried red chillies, broken into pieces
½ tsp black gram (urad dal)
2 tsp scraped (grated) coconut
1 medium-sized onion or 3 rose onions, sliced
1 sprig curry leaves
½ tsp tamarind pulp
½ tsp salt

METHOD

1. Heat ghee and sauté dried chillies and black gram. Add scraped coconut, onions and curry leaves. Cook for about a minute or two, tossing continuously to prevent burning.
2. Add the leaves. Allow the water from the leaves to be absorbed. Remove from stove.
3. Add tamarind pulp and salt.
4. Grind the mixture fine.
5. Serve with rice.

Ginger Chambal

Inji Chambal

Thumb-sized piece ginger, chopped
3 tsp ghee
2 green chillies, sliced
6–8 curry leaves
3 small rose onions or 1 medium-sized onion, chopped
1 tbsp scraped (grated) coconut
½ tsp salt
½ tsp tamarind pulp

METHOD

1. Heat ghee and sauté ginger, green chillies, curry leaves and onions.
2. Remove from stove.
3. Grind together sautéed ingredients, scraped coconut, salt and tamarind pulp.

Coconut Chambal

Thengaapu Chambal

½ cup coconut scraped (grated)
1 tsp tamarind pulp
4 dried red chillies
Salt to taste
4 tsp oil
¼ tsp mustard seeds
¼ tsp split black gram (urad dal) } *for seasoning*
1 sprig curry leaves

METHOD

1. Grind coconut, tamarind pulp, dried chillies and salt, fine.
2. Heat oil and fry mustard seeds, black gram and curry leaves.
3. Add to coconut mixture and mix well.

Green Chilli Chambal

Pachai Milaaggaai Chambal

6 green chillies
3 cloves garlic
1 tbsp grated coconut
1 tsp tamarind pulp
Salt to taste
¼ tsp mustard seeds
¼ tsp split black gram (urad dal)
A tiny piece asafoetida or a pinch powdered asafoetida
3 tsp oil

METHOD

1. Fry all the ingredients in the oil on a moderate flame. Set aside to cool.
2. Grind to a fine paste. Add water if necessary and mix well.

Only a tiny bit of this piquant chambal is required to impart that pungent taste to a rice or porridge.

Sesame Chambal (Sesame Arayal)

Ellu Chambal

10 dessertspoons white sesame seeds
3 tsp gingelly oil
5 dried red chilles
10 dessertspoons grated coconut
10–14 curry leaves
1½ bouquets garlic (about 15 cloves)
1 dessertspoon peppercorns
4 tsp tamarind pulp
1¼ tsp salt

METHOD

1. Heat gingelly oil. Fry sesame seeds and dried chillies. Set aside.
2. Roast grated coconut and curry leaves.
3. Mix all together and pound or grind.

4. Add garlic, salt, peppercorns and tamarind.
5. Continue to grind till all ingredients are well blended.

Ellu chambal keeps well and is a delicious accompaniment to thosai or hot rice. Store it in a jar till required.

Amma's nephew had come to visit us from Malaysia. All the relatives from the other villages came to see him and to invite him to their homes. Nagalingam Maama, Amma's cousin brother, was known to us as 'Kulari Maama' on account of the fact that he used to shout when talking. I later learnt that this was because he was deaf in one ear. Kulari Maama also came on his bicycle to visit Athaan.

He brought a bottle of ellu chambal wrapped in the thundu of his veti [veshti] set (the white shawl of a dhoti set). He shouted for my mother to bring the rice 'hot-hot', straight from the pot on a plate. He undid the bundle and unscrewing the lid served himself the ellu chambal on the rice. Athaan needed no second bidding. He sat down, and almost ignoring all the other dishes Amma had prepared, mixed the ellu chambal with his hot rice and ate a mouthful. He closed his eyes, threw his head back and let out a great breath.

"I have been dreaming of this ellu chambal all the way on the boat, Maama," he said his eyes wet with the pungency of the chambal as well as something else from his heart.

S. Arumugam: "Letters from Jaffna"

Hot Coconut Chambal

Uraipu Thengaapu Chutney

1 cup grated coconut
7 or 8 dried red chillies, soaked in water
Salt to taste
4 or 5 thin slices of fresh ginger
1 sprig curry leaves
1 medium-sized onion, chopped
½ tsp tamarind pulp or 1 tsp lime/lemon juice

1tsp ghee or gingelly oil
1 small onion, sliced
1 dried red chilli, broken into small pieces   } for seasoning
¼ tsp mustard seeds
¼ tsp split black gram (urad dal)
A few curry leaves

METHOD

1. Drain dried chillies. Grind together with salt.
2. Add grated coconut and ginger slices. Grind together.
3. Add curry leaves and onions.
4. Remove from grinder and add tamarind pulp or lime/lemon juice.
5. Heat ghee or oil in a pan. Add the sliced onions and sauté for a minute before adding dried chillies, mustard seeds, black gram and curry leaves.
6. Add to coconut chambal and mix before serving.

This is an excellent accompaniment to thosai and idli.

Chutneys

Chutneys are popular for their hot-sour-sweet content, and serve to set off the pungent curries—so balancing the different tastes of each. Chutneys keep well and so can be made and stored.

Onion Chutney

Venggaya Chutney

3 medium-sized onions, chopped (if using rose onions, sliced)
3 dessertspoons gingelly oil
1½ teaspoons split black gram (urad dal)
2 dried red chillies, broken into pieces
1 dessertspoon grated coconut
1 tsp tamarind pulp
1 sprig curry leaves
½ tsp salt
¼ cup water
½ tsp mustard seeds
1 tsp sugar

METHOD

1. Heat ½ teaspoon oil and sauté 1 teaspoon split black gram and dried chillies.
2. Add grated coconut and toss together. Remove from stove.
3. Heat 1 dessertspoon oil and fry onions till light golden.
4. Add fried black gram and chillies to onions.
5. Add tamarind pulp, curry leaves and salt. Toss together.

6. Remove from stove.
7. Grind all the above ingredients together. Remove from grinder and add water.
8. Heat remaining oil in a pan. Sauté remaining black gram and mustard seeds.
9. Add ground ingredients and sugar.
10. Bring mixture to boil. Stir thoroughly and remove from flame at once.

Pumpkin Chutney

Puusanikkaai Chutney

2 cups pumpkin pieces
A whole bouquet of garlic (at least 10–12 cloves)
Thumb-sized piece ginger
1½ cups vinegar
¾ cup sugar
1 tsp chilli powder
¼ tsp salt
1 tbsp sultanas

METHOD

1. Cook the pumpkin pieces in a little water till soft. Mash.
2. Pound garlic and ginger together, fine.
3. Place vinegar, sugar, chilli powder, salt and pounded ginger-garlic in a pan (not brass or aluminium).
4. Bring to boil. Add mashed pumpkin and cook till chutney thickens.
5. Remove from stove and add sultanas. Mix well.

Tomato Chutney

Thakkaali Chutney

1 kg tomatoes, chopped
1½ dessertspoons oil
½ tsp cumin seeds
1 tsp mustard seeds
1 tsp grated ginger
3 green chillies, chopped fine
1 sprig curry leaves
¼ tsp turmeric powder
½ cup jaggery pieces (or 1 dessertspoon honey)

METHOD

1. Grind tomatoes.
2. Heat oil. Fry cumin seeds, mustard seeds and ginger till the seeds splutter.
3. Fry chopped green chillies and curry leaves.
4. Add ground tomato, turmeric powder and boil till thick.
5. Add jaggery or honey.
6. Mix well and remove.
7. Allow to cool and store till ready to use.

Date and Tomato Chutney

Perichampala Thakkali Chutney

4 tomatoes, peeled and chopped
¼ cup pitted dates, chopped fine
6 dried red chillies, broken into pieces
Thumb-sized piece of ginger
10 cloves garlic
¾ cup vinegar
3 tsp sultanas
½ cup sugar
½ tsp salt

METHOD

1. Blanch and chop the peeled tomatoes.
2. Grind together, dried chillies, ginger and garlic. Add a little vinegar to aid grinding process.
3. Place vinegar, tomatoes, dates and sultanas in a pan (not brass or aluminium) and bring to boil.
4. Add sugar, salt and ground ingredients.
5. Mix well. Cook further till chutney thickens. Remove from stove and set aside to cool.
6. Store and use as required.

Chutney Podi

1 cup Bengal gram (channa dal)
¼ cup split black gram (urad dal)
¼ cup white sesame seeds
2 dessertspoons gingelly oil

5–8 *curry leaves*
1 cup *grated coconut*
A tiny piece asafoetida
10 *dried red chillies, cut fine*
½ tsp *salt*
1 tsp *mustard seeds*
1 tsp *tamarind pulp*
1 *onion, chopped fine*

METHOD

1. Roast Bengal gram, black gram and sesame seeds, separately.
2. Separately grind each, fine.
3. Heat gingelly oil. Fry curry leaves and grated coconut and remove from oil.
4. Fry asafoetida and remove from oil.
5. Fry dried chillies and remove from oil.
6. Add mustard seeds. Fry till they pop. Remove from oil.
7. Mix curry leaves, coconut, asafoetida, dried chillies, mustard seeds and tamarind pulp. Pound or grind well.
8. Add ground Bengal gram, black gram, sesame seeds, salt and chopped onion. Pound or grind to blend all the ingredients.
9. Store till needed.

This is a perfect accompaniment to idlis and thosais.

Thosai Podi

1 cup *Bengal gram (channa dal)*
1 cup *split black gram (urad dal)*
1 cup *sesame seeds*
1 cup *curry leaves*
Thumb-nail sized piece asafoetida
10 *dried red chillies, broken into pieces*
1 tsp *salt*

METHOD

1. Separately roast Bengal gram, black gram, sesame seeds, curry leaves, asafoetida, dried chillies and salt. Set aside to cool.
2. When all ingredients are completely cool, grind together, fine.
3. Store till required.

Vegetables

Bitter Gourd Curry
Drumstick Curry
Long Beans Curry
Green Banana (Ash Plantain) White Curry

Snake Gourd White Curry
Fried Brinjal Curry
Coconut Milk Brinjal Curry
Green Banana (Ash Plantain) Skin Curry

Fried Dal Curry
Dry Potato Curry
Potato White Curry
Okra (Ladies' Fingers) Curry

Pumpkin Curry
Yam Curry
Bottle Gourd White Curry
Jackfruit Curry

Long Beans and Jackfruit Seeds Curry
Beetroot Curry
Breadfruit Dry Curry
Sundanggaai Curry
Vegetarian "Charakku" Curry

Mango Curry
Garlic Curry
Fenugreek Seeds Curry
Aviyal

Mixed Vegetable Korma
Mashed Spinach
Hibiscus Leaf Varai
Carrot Varai

Potato Fry
Jackfruit Seed Fry
Brinjal/Aubergine Fry
Green Banana (Ash Plantain) Fry

Tapioca Fry
Plantain Flower Cutlets
Potato Cutlets
Vegetable Cutlets
Jackfruit Seed Cutlets

Bitter Gourd Curry

Paavakkaai Kari

500 gm bitter gourd, seeds removed and flesh cut into small pieces
Coconut water (from 2 coconuts or 3 cups water with 2 tsp salt)
2 tbsp oil
10 small red onions or 1 large onion, chopped
4 green chillies
Tamarind pulp or paste to taste
4 tsp curry powder
1½ tsp salt
8 tbsp thick coconut milk
1 tsp sugar
1 sprig curry leaves

METHOD

1. Place bitter gourd in coconut water and bring to boil to remove bitterness. (Alternatively, soak in salted water for ½ an hour)
2. In another pan, heat oil. Fry chopped onions and green chillies till onions turn golden brown.
3. Add bitter gourd pieces and stir to mix.
4. Add tamarind pulp/paste, curry powder, salt and coconut milk.
5. Allow to cook and then simmer. Add sugar and curry leaves and remove from heat.

All dishes made from bitter gourd (bitter melon) are highly recommended for diabetics.

Drumstick Curry

Murungakkaai Kari

500 gm or 4 large drumsticks
4 tbsp oil
1 tsp fenugreek seeds
10 small onions or 1 large onion, chopped
10 cloves garlic
3 green chillies
4 tsp curry powder
1 tsp salt
1½ cups water
6 tbsp coconut milk
1 tsp tamarind pulp or paste
1 sprig curry leaves

METHOD

1. Cut drumsticks into about 7 cm pieces and split down the middle.
2. Heat oil. Add fenugreek seeds and fry till golden brown.
3. Add onions, garlic and green chillies. Fry till golden brown.
4. Add drumsticks and mix with fried ingredients.
5. Add curry powder, salt and water.
6. Cover with a lid and cook till drumsticks are tender.
7. Add coconut milk and tamarind pulp/paste. Stir mixture through gently.
8. Allow to simmer.
9. Add curry leaves and remove from heat.

The kelor or drumstick tree is a popular garden tree in both India as well as Sri Lanka and the Tamil areas. Known as Moringa oleifera, it is becoming increasingly popular for its medicinal value. The leaves of the Moringa tree are rich in vitamins A and C and a cupful of leaves provides more than the recommended daily requirement. They are rich in calcium and iron and are also a very good source of phosphorus.

The drumstick fruits are in long pods (hence the name) and are extremely popular among Tamils, as are the leaves. Being a rich source of protein, drumstick is cooked as part of a new mother's special diet.

All parts of the tree are useful—the fruit, the leaves, the flowers—which are made into delicious, nutritious 'vadaham' or crispy snacks.

Long Beans Curry

Paithanggaai Kari

500 gm long beans, cut into 2–3 cm pieces
2 tbsp cooking oil
1 medium-sized onion, chopped
2 green chillies, sliced
1 tsp salt
4 tsp curry powder
1 cup water
3 tbsp coconut milk
½ tsp tamarind pulp or paste
6–8 curry leaves

Method

1. Heat oil in a pan. Add onions and chillies. Cook for a minute or so, till onion turns soft and slightly golden.
2. Add long beans and cook for another 2–3 minutes.
3. Add salt, curry powder and water. Cook till the water is absorbed, turning mixture over a couple of times.
4. Add coconut milk and tamarind pulp/paste, and fold in gently. Remove from the stove.

Green Banana (Ash Plantain) White Curry

Vaalakkaai Paal Kari

3 large ash plantains
1 tbsp scraped (grated) coconut
A pinch turmeric powder
2 medium-sized onions or 5 small rose onions, sliced
2 green chillies, sliced
6–8 curry leaves
¾ tsp salt
1½ cups thick coconut milk
1 tsp roasted cumin powder

Method

1. Skin ash plantains and cut into cubes.
2. Smear with scraped coconut to remove any stains.
3. Add turmeric and mix well.

4. Cook plantains, onions, green chillies, curry leaves and salt, together in a pan.
5. When cooked, add coconut milk. Bring to boil once. Remove from stove.
6. Add roasted cumin powder and mix well.

Snake Gourd White Curry

Pidalanggaai Kari

500 gm snake gourd
1 tsp chilli powder
6 small rose onions or 1 large onion, sliced
2 green chillies, sliced
6–8 curry leaves
½ tsp salt
½ tsp turmeric powder
2 ½ cups coconut milk
1 tsp roasted cumin seed powder

METHOD

1. Scrape outer skin of snake gourd and slit into two. Remove all seeds and slice.
2. Cook together in a pan, snake gourd, chilli powder, onions, green chillies, curry leaves, salt, turmeric powder and coconut milk.
3. Cook till the curry appears a little oily. Remove from stove.
4. Add roasted cumin seed powder and mix well.

Fried Brinjal Curry

Kaththarikkaai Kari

2 brinjal/aubergines, sliced into 2 inch pieces
Oil for frying
1 medium-sized onion, chopped
3 green chillies
1 tbsp gingelly oil or ghee
1 tsp fenugreek seeds
1 sprig curry leaves
1½ tbsp curry powder
2 tsp tamarind pulp
½ tsp salt
3 tbsp coconut milk

METHOD

1. Heat oil in a pan and deep-fry pieces of brinjal. Drain on absorbent paper.
2. Fry onions and green chillies till onions begin to brown. Remove from oil and add to brinjal.
3. Heat 1 tablespoon gingelly oil or ghee.
4. Add fenugreek seeds, curry leaves, curry powder, tamarind and salt.
5. Add coconut milk and, as it begins to boil, add brinjal.
6. Stir till liquid reduces. Remove from stove.

Coconut Milk Brinjal Curry

Kaththarikkaai Paal Curry

1 brinjal/aubergine (2 cups brinjal pieces)
1 green chilli, sliced
1 small onion, chopped
½ tsp salt (or to taste)
½ tsp turmeric powder
½ cup water
½ cup coconut milk
1 sprig curry leaves
1 tsp lime/lemon juice

METHOD

1. Put brinjal, green chillies, chopped onions, salt and turmeric powder in a pot. Half cover the vegetables with water. Cover and cook.
2. When cooked and water has reduced, stir well. Add coconut milk and curry leaves.
3. Cook for another five minutes, tossing occasionally.
4. Remove. Add lime/lemon juice and mix well.

Green Banana (Ash Plantain) Skin Curry

Vaalakkaai Thol Kari

Skin of 3 or 4 ash plantains
1 green chilli, chopped fine
1 dessertspoon chopped onions
½ tsp salt

1 dessertspoon thick coconut milk
1 tsp tamarind pulp
1 dessertspoon chilli powder
½ tsp cumin powder
½ tsp coriander powder
1 sprig curry leaves
1 tsp oil
¼ tsp mustard seeds
¼ tsp split black gram (urad dal)   } for seasoning
1 dried chilli, broken into small pieces

METHOD

1. Peel the green outer skin of the banana. Cut the white pithy part into thin strips about an inch long.
2. In a pot, put plantain skin strips, chopped green chilli, chopped onion and salt.
3. Add water to almost cover the mixture in the pot. Cover and cook till well done.
4. Uncover. Add thick coconut milk, tamarind pulp and chilli powder. Stir well to mix.
5. When water has reduced and curry has thickened, add cumin and coriander powder, and curry leaves. Mix well. Allow to cook for a further three to five minutes.
6. Stir and remove from stove.
7. In a small pan, heat oil. Add mustard seeds, black gram and dried chillies. Sauté.
8. Add to the curry.

Fried Dal Curry

Poritha Paruppu Kari

1 cup split green gram (moong dal) or split red gram (tuar dal), roasted
¾ tsp salt
Oil for frying
1 green chilli, chopped fine
1 medium-sized onion, chopped fine
1½ tsp chilli powder
1 tsp charakku curry powder or
    ½ tsp ground cumin, ½ tsp coriander powder
1 inch piece cinnamon
1 cup coconut milk (medium)
1 sprig curry leaves
½ tsp lime/lemon juice

METHOD

1. Soak gram in water for 2 hours. Drain and grind coarsely, so that it has a grainy texture. Add ¼ teaspoon salt.
2. Form little flat patties.
3. Steam the patties. Once firm, remove and lay out on a plate to cool.
4. Heat oil and deep-fry patties till golden. Drain on absorbent paper.
5. Deep-fry green chillies and onions till golden. Drain.
6. Toss together and cook fried onions and green chillies, chilli powder, charakku powder, cinnamon, fried patties, coconut milk and ½ teaspoon salt.
7. When gravy thickens, add curry leaves. Stir and remove from flame.
8. Add lime/lemon juice and mix well.

Dry Potato Curry

Urulakkilangu Pirattal

5 potatoes, peeled and cut into large cubes
1½ dessertspoons oil
1 tsp mustard seeds
¼ tsp fenugreek seeds
½ tsp fennel seed powder
1 medium-sized onion, chopped
6–8 curry leaves
1 green chilli
Thumb-sized piece of ginger
1 cup coconut milk
½ cup water
½ tsp cumin seed powder
½ tsp coriander powder
A small piece cinnamon
1 tsp chilli powder
1 tsp salt

METHOD

1. Heat oil in a pan. Add mustard and fenugreek seeds, fennel seed powder, chopped onion and curry leaves. Fry till onions turn golden.
2. Add potatoes, green chillies, ginger, coconut milk, water, cumin seed powder and coriander powder, cinnamon, chilli powder and salt.
3. Cook till liquid is absorbed. Stir for a minute or so.
4. Remove from flame.

Potato White Curry

Urulakkilangu Paal Kari

4 potatoes
2 green chillies, chopped
1 medium-sized onion, chopped
6–7 cloves garlic
A pinch turmeric powder
¼ tsp fenugreek seeds
½ tsp salt
6–8 curry leaves
¼ cup thick coconut milk

METHOD

1. Peel and cube potatoes.
2. Place in a pan with all the ingredients except the coconut milk. Stir mixture occasionally, to prevent burning.
3. When potatoes are soft, add coconut milk.
4. Stir till curry boils again. Remove from flame.

Okra (Ladies' Fingers) Curry

Vendikkaai Kari

"Meat for vegetarians, that's what vendikkaai is! Eat it as often as you can and you can leave out meat all together!" said the very nutrition-conscious Mrs Esther Bastian Pillay who lived to be a healthy 98.

10 tender okra (ladies' fingers)
2 green chillies, sliced
1 medium-sized onion, sliced
¼ tsp fenugreek seeds
½ tsp chilli powder
½ tsp salt
5–8 curry leaves
¼ cup water
¼ cup thick coconut milk

METHOD

1. Wash okra and dry with a dishcloth. Cut into inch-long pieces.
2. In a pan, put okra pieces, green chillies, sliced onion, fenugreek seeds, chilli powder, salt and curry leaves. Mix together.

3. Add water. Cook till water is almost absorbed.
4. Stir the curry and add coconut milk. Cook for another two or three minutes.
5. Once liquid is reduced remove from stove.

Pumpkin Curry

Puusanikkaai Kari

4 cups pumpkin pieces
1 medium-sized onion, chopped
1 or 3 green chillies (to taste), sliced
5–6 cloves garlic, crushed
¼ tsp chilli powder
½ tsp salt
¾ cup water
¼ tsp cumin seed powder
¼ cup thick coconut milk
6–8 curry leaves
1 tsp oil
¼ tsp mustard seeds
¼ tsp split black gram (urad dal)
1 dried red chilli, broken into small pieces

} *for seasoning*

METHOD

1. Put pumpkin pieces, chopped onion, green chillies, garlic, chilli powder, salt and water, in a pot. Bring to boil and cook till pumpkin is tender.
2. Add cumin seed powder, coconut milk and curry leaves. Mix well. When liquid has been absorbed, mix again and remove from flame.
3. In a small pan, heat oil. Add mustard seeds, black gram and dried chillies. Sauté.
4. Add to pumpkin curry.

Yam Curry

Karunai Kilangu Kari

This yam is round and bulbous with a dried or 'fried' look on the outside. Its body is a lovely pale orange. Its taste is compared to that of meat and some preparations treat it in a similar manner when cooking it as a dry 'pirattal' curry.

500 gm yam (karunai kilangu), peeled and cut into cubes
1 green chilli, sliced

¼ tsp fenugreek seeds
1 medium-sized onion, sliced
1 cup coconut milk
1–2 tsp chilli powder
¼ tsp cumin seed powder
¼ tsp coriander powder
¾ tsp salt
1 sprig curry leaves
A small piece cinnamon
Oil for frying

METHOD

1. Deep-fry yam cubes and drain on absorbent paper.
2. Fry green chillies, fenugreek and sliced onion. Drain and add to fried yam.
3. In a pan, put yam, green chillies and onions.
4. Add coconut milk, chilli powder, cumin seed powder, coriander powder, salt, curry leaves and cinnamon. Cook till liquid reduces a little. Simmer over a low flame for another three minutes.
5. Remove from flame.

Bottle Gourd White Curry

Churakkaai Paal Kari

Churakkaai is a popular vegetable for anyone with a fluid retention problem.

500 gm bottle gourd, peeled and cubed
1 green chilli, sliced
1 large onion, sliced
¼ tsp fenugreek seeds
½ tsp salt
¼ cup thick coconut milk
1 sprig curry leaves
1 tsp lime/lemon juice

METHOD

1. Put in a pan, bottle gourd pieces, green chillies, sliced onion, fenugreek seeds and salt.
2. Cover and cook over a low flame, till tender.
3. When cooked, uncover. Add coconut milk. Add curry leaves once liquid has thickened and mix well.
4. Remove from flame. Add lime/lemon juice and mix well.

Jackfruit Curry

Pilaakkaai Kari

500 gm flesh and seed of young jackfruit, chopped
1½ dessertspoons oil
½ tsp mustard seeds
less than ¼ tsp fenugreek seeds
1 sprig curry leaves
1 green chilli, sliced
1 medium-sized onion, chopped
10 cloves garlic, crushed or pounded in a pestle
½ tsp ground pepper
1 cup water
1 tsp curry powder
1 tsp salt
½ cup coconut milk

METHOD

1. Heat oil in a pan. Fry mustard seeds, fenugreek seeds and curry leaves.
2. Add green chillies, chopped onion, garlic and pepper.
3. Add jackfruit pieces and water. Cook till jackfruit is tender.
4. Mix curry powder and salt in the coconut milk and add to the pan.
5. Mix well and cook for a further five minutes.

Long Beans and Jackfruit Seeds Curry

Paithanggaai Pilaakottai Kari

"Even if there is nothing else, I could eat rice just with this!" is a common exclamation when this dish is eaten. This combination of long beans and jackfruit seeds is one of the most popular dishes in Tamil cuisine.

500 gm long beans
200 gm jackfruit seeds
4 green chillies, sliced
1 large onion, chopped
½ tsp salt
1 sprig curry leaves
1 tbsp curry powder
5 dessertspoons coconut milk
½ cup water

1 tsp oil
¼ tsp mustard seeds
¼ tsp split black gram (urad dal) } for seasoning
2 dried red chillies, broken into small pieces

METHOD

1. Cook long beans, jackfruit seeds, green chillies, chopped onions, salt and curry leaves in water.
2. When liquid has reduced, add curry powder and coconut milk.
3. Cook till liquid has reduced again and curry has thickened.
4. Remove from stove.
5. In a small pan, heat oil. Add mustard seeds, black gram and dried chillies. Sauté.
6. Pour on to the curry.

Beetroot Curry

2 cups beetroot, cut into inch-long, fine strips
2 green chillies, chopped
1 medium-sized onion, chopped
½ cup water
½ tsp salt
¼ tsp chilli powder
1 dessertspoon thick coconut milk
¼ tsp cumin powder
1 sprig curry leaves
1 tsp lime/lemon juice

METHOD

1. In a pan cook beetroot, green chillies, chopped onion, water, salt and chilli powder.
2. When liquid has reduced, add coconut milk, cumin powder and curry leaves.
3. Mix well together. When liquid has reduced again, remove from flame.
4. Add lime/lemon juice and mix well.

Breadfruit Dry Curry

Eerapilaakkaai Thuvattal

2 cups breadfruit flesh, chopped
½ tsp salt (or to taste)

¼ tsp turmeric powder
1½ cups water
3 dessertspoons oil
½ tsp mustard seeds
1 medium-sized onion, chopped fine
1 tsp chilli powder
6–8 garlic cloves, crushed
1 sprig curry leaves, chopped fine

METHOD

1. Boil breadfruit pieces, salt and turmeric powder in water.
2. When cooked, remove.
3. Heat oil in a pan. Fry mustard seeds, chopped onion, chilli powder, garlic and curry leaves.
4. Add breadfruit pieces.
5. Lower flame, mix well and cook for another 4–5 minutes, tossing continuously to prevent burning.
6. Remove when done.

Sundanggaai Curry

500 gm sundanggaai (Solanum pubescens)
1 dessertspoon oil
¼ tsp mustard seeds
5 or 6 curry leaves
2 green chillies, chopped fine
1 medium-sized onion, chopped
2 tsp curry powder
½ tsp salt
1 tsp tamarind pulp
½ cup coconut milk

METHOD

1. Prepare sundanggaai by flattening each on a cutting board and removing seeds.
2. Heat oil in a pan. Fry mustard seeds and curry leaves.
3. Add green chillies and chopped onion. Fry a little.
4. Add sundanggaai and cook till soft.
5. Mix curry powder, salt and tamarind pulp in coconut milk.
6. Add to sundanggaai.
7. Cook till the curry thickens and remove from stove.

Vegetarian "Charakku" Curry

Pathiya Curry

This preparation is usually given to lactating mothers. Chilly is reduced to just one and the other spices aid digestion and recovery.

200 gm young drumsticks
   (other options are young brinjals, young ash plantain or potatoes)
3½ tsp coriander seeds
½ tsp cumin seeds
½ tsp pepper
1 dried red chilli
10 small onions or 1 large onion, chopped
¼ tsp fenugreek seeds
a pinch turmeric powder
6 garlic cloves
Salt to taste
2 cups water
½ tsp tamarind pulp
6–8 curry leaves
1 tbsp thick coconut milk

METHOD

1. Grind together finely, coriander and cumin seeds, pepper and dried chilli.
2. Split the drumsticks into halves. (If using other vegetables, cut into bite-size pieces.)
3. Cover and cook vegetables of choice with chopped onions, fenugreek seeds, turmeric, garlic and salt, in 1½ cups water.
4. Mix ground ingredients and tamarind pulp in half cup water.
5. Add to pan, together with curry leaves and coconut milk.

Note: See "Chicken Pathiya Curry" for a non-vegetarian preparation.

Mango Curry

Maanggaai Kari

4 unripe mangoes, peeled and cut into pieces
1½ tsp salt
4 cups water
½ tsp mustard seeds
3½ dessertspoons oil
2 large onions chopped (or 20 rose onions)

5 green chillies, chopped
1 sprig curry leaves
8 cloves garlic, sliced
Thumb-sized piece ginger, chopped fine
3 dessertspoons vinegar
3 tsp curry powder
1½ cups light coconut milk
1 stick cinnamon
4 tsp sugar

METHOD

1. Rub mango pieces with 1 teaspoon salt. Soak mangoes in water for about an hour.
2. Heat a pan and toss mustard seeds in it till they pop.
3. Add the oil immediately. When heated, add chopped onions, green chillies, curry leaves, garlic and ginger. Fry till onions turn golden.
4. Add mango pieces and ½ teaspoon salt. Toss together to coat mangoes with fried ingredients.
5. Add vinegar. Allow to boil together.
6. Dissolve curry powder in coconut milk. Add to pan.
7. Add cinnamon stick and sugar. Mix together and lower the flame. Simmer for a while till the curry thickens a little. Remove.

Garlic Curry

Ulli Kari

2 cups cloves of garlic, peeled and halved
2½ dessertspoons oil
1 tsp fenugreek seeds
20 rose onions or 3 medium-sized onions, quartered and sliced
5 green chillies, chopped
1 sprig curry leaves
2 tsp salt
2–3 tsp tamarind pulp
3 tsp curry powder
2 cups coconut milk

METHOD

1. Heat oil in a pan. Add fenugreek seeds and fry till golden.
2. Add sliced onions, garlic, green chillies and curry leaves.
3. Mix salt, tamarind pulp and curry powder to coconut milk.
4. Add to mixture and cook through. After the first boil reduce flame and simmer till curry thickens.

Fenugreek Seeds Curry

Venthiya Kulambu

This particular curry is a favourite amongst the Tamils. It keeps well and is the mainstay of a vegetarian meal. Eaten with puttu or string hoppers, it draws ecstatic appreciation from the diner. Sometimes vegetables such as drumstick or fried slices of brinjal (aubergine) are added.

1 dessertspoon fenugreek seeds
2 dessertspoons oil
10 rose onions, sliced or 1 large onion, quartered and sliced
20 cloves garlic, halved
2 green chillies, sliced
1 sprig curry leaves
2 dessertspoons tamarind pulp
2 dessertspoons curry powder
½ tsp turmeric powder
½ cup water
¼ tsp salt (or to taste)
1 dessertspoon coconut milk

METHOD

1. Heat oil in a pan. Add fenugreek seeds. Allow to turn golden (fry for just half a minute).
2. Add sliced onion, garlic, green chillies and curry leaves.
3. As soon as onions turn golden, add tamarind pulp, curry powder, turmeric powder, water and salt.
4. Bring to boil.
5. Add coconut milk. Simmer for about 10 minutes.
6. Remove from stove.

Aviyal

Aviyal

Thought to be a traditional dish from Kerala, the Jaffna Tamils have adopted aviyal as part of their cuisine.

500 gm mixed vegetables, cut into cubes
(Recommended vegetables: ash plantain, pumpkin, potato, brinjal/aubergine, snake gourd, carrot, cauliflour, young jackfruit. Vegetables used should be firm, not pulpy.)
½ tsp cumin seed
1 cup fresh or dessicated coconut
½ tsp uncooked rice   } grind to a fine powder
8 green chillies
1 tsp split black gram (urad dal)
1½ cups yoghurt
3 slices green mango
2½ cups water
2 tsp salt
2 tsp ghee or gingelly oil
1 tsp mustard seeds
1 medium-sized onion, chopped fine
3 dried red chillies, broken into small pieces

METHOD

1. Mix ground ingredients and yoghurt. Set aside.
2. Place vegetables and mango slices in a pan. Add water and cook for 10 minutes.
3. Add salt and cook for a further 5 minutes, stirring slowly, till almost all the water has been absorbed.
4. Add yoghurt and spices mixture and fold in gently.
5. Heat oil in another pan. Add mustard seeds, chopped onion and dried chillies. Add to cooked vegetables. Stir in and remove from heat.

Mixed Vegetable Korma

Marakari Kurma

Korma is a dish popular among Muslims. Its creamy texture and subtle flavour makes it a popular choice for those who do not like hot food.

3 cups mixed vegetables, cut into bite-size pieces (any firm vegetable, carrot, cauliflower, young jackfruit or ash plantain, can be used)
½ tsp cumin seeds

1 small piece cinnamon stick
2 cloves
3 cardamom pods
1 tsp poppy seeds
Thumb-sized piece ginger
20 cashew nuts
5 cloves garlic
1 dessertspoon grated coconut
3 dessertspoons ghee
½ tsp ground pepper
1 tsp salt
1 cup water
4 tomatoes, chopped
4 potatoes (medium-sized), cut into cubes
10 rose onions, sliced or 1 large onion, quartered and sliced
1½ tsp white mustard seeds
3 green chillies, sliced
1 rampé (pandanus) leaf
1 sprig curry leaves
½ tsp curry powder
3 dessertspoons thick yoghurt
1 tsp lime/lemon juice

METHOD

1. Roast cumin seeds, cinnamon stick, cloves and cardamom. Pound or dry grind fine.
2. Wet grind poppy seeds, ginger, cashew nuts, garlic and grated coconut.
3. In a heavy pan, heat 1 dessertspoon ghee. Add all the chopped vegetables except tomatoes and potatoes. Put in ground pepper, and ½ teaspoon salt. Toss and add ½ cup water and cover. Cook till vegetables are tender. Remove into a bowl.
4. In a pan, heat 1 dessertspoon ghee. Add chopped tomatoes, ½ teaspoon salt , ½ cup water and potatoes. Toss together and cook till potatoes are tender. Remove and add to the bowl of cooked vegetables.
5. Wash pan. Heat remaining ghee. Add onions, mustard seeds, green chillies, rampé leaf, curry leaves. Toss till the onions become transparent.
6. Add curry powder and dry ground spices (see step 1 above). Mix well.
7. Add cooked vegetables, yoghurt and remaining salt. Toss together well. Simmer on a low flame.
8. When vegetables are well blended with spices, stir thoroughly and remove from stove.
9. Add lime/lemon juice and stir once more.

Mashed Spinach

Keera Kadaiyal

A bunch of spinach leaves, washed and cut into large pieces
2 tsp oil
1 tsp chopped onion
3 cloves garlic, crushed
2 dried red chillies, broken into pieces
5–7 curry leaves
¼ tsp mustard seeds
2 green chillies, chopped fine
¼ tsp turmeric powder
Salt to taste
2 dessertspoons water
½ tsp lime/lemon juice

METHOD

1. Heat oil. Add chopped onion. Sautè.
2. Add crushed garlic, dried chillies, curry leaves and mustard seeds.
3. Fry for a minute.
4. Add spinach, green chillies, turmeric, salt and water.
5. When spinach is cooked and softened, mash it a little with the back of a wooden ladle.
6. Add lime/lemon juice. (This detracts from the nutritional value of the spinach but adds to its flavour.)

Hibiscus Leaf Varai

Semparathilai Varai

2 cups young hibiscus leaves (the light coloured young leaves)
3 tsp oil
1 medium-sized onion, chopped
2 dried red chillies, broken into pieces
¼ tsp chopped ginger
¼ tsp mustard seeds
5–7 curry leaves, chopped fine
2 dessertspoons grated coconut
Salt to taste

METHOD

1. Cut hibiscus leaves fine.
2. Heat oil. Fry chopped onion, dried chillies and ginger.
3. Add mustard seeds. When they pop, add hibiscus leaves and curry leaves.
4. Add grated coconut and salt to taste. Stir till leaves are cooked. Remove from stove.

Carrot Varai

2 cups finely grated carrot
3 tsp oil
1 medium-sized onion, chopped
2 dried red chillies, broken into pieces
¼ tsp chopped ginger
¼ tsp mustard seeds
5–7 curry leaves, chopped fine
¼ tsp turmeric powder
¼ tsp chilli powder
2 dessertspoons grated coconut
Salt to taste
½ tsp lime/lemon juice

METHOD

1. Heat oil. Fry chopped onion, dried chillies and ginger.
2. Add mustard seeds and curry leaves.
3. Add carrot, turmeric powder, chilli powder and grated coconut.
4. Add salt and toss for about two minutes.
5. Remove from stove and sprinkle lime/lemon juice.

Potato Fry

Urulakkilangu Poriyal

4 potatoes, cut into very small cubes
1 tsp chilli powder
½ tsp turmeric powder
½ tsp salt
4 dessertspoons oil
1 medium-sized onion, chopped

METHOD

1. Marinade potatoes with chilli powder, turmeric and salt, for ten minutes.
2. Heat oil in a pan. Add cubed potatoes.
3. When half cooked, add chopped onion.
4. Turn and fry continuously (add more oil if required).
5. When potatoes are well cooked and onions golden, turn off stove and remove.

Jackfruit Seed Fry

Pilaakottai Poriyal

1 cup   jackfruit seeds
1 tsp   chilli powder
¼ tsp   turmeric powder
¼ tsp   salt
3–4 dessertspoons   oil

METHOD

1. Boil jackfruit seeds. Drain water when cooked.
2. Skin and cut into small cubes.
3. Marinade with chilli, turmeric and salt for about 15 minutes.
4. Heat oil in a pan. Fry jackfruit seeds till golden. Remove

Brinjal/Aubergine Poriyal

Kaththarikkaai Poriyal

2 cups   tender brinjal/aubergine
1 tsp   chilli powder
1 tsp   rice flour
½ tsp   salt
Oil for frying

METHOD

1. Marinade the brinjal pieces with chilli powder, rice flour and salt.
2. Heat oil in a pan.
3. Deep-fry brinjal pieces.
4. Drain as soon as pieces turn golden.

Green Banana (Ash Plantain) Fry

Vaalakkaai Poriyal

3 ash plantains, peeled and cubed
1 tsp chilli powder
½ tsp salt
1 medium-sized onion, chopped
1 sprig curry leaves
¼ cup oil

METHOD

1. Marinade plantain pieces with chilli powder and salt for about 10–15 minutes.
2. Heat oil in a pan. Fry plantain pieces till golden. Check a piece to be sure it is cooked.
3. Add chopped onion and curry leaves. Toss and stir till all pieces are cooked and onions are golden.
4. Remove from stove.

Tapioca Fry

Maravallikilangu Poriyal

1 whole tapioca
½ tsp salt
1 cup water
Oil for frying
1 tsp chilli powder
1 dessertspoon ghee or preferred cooking oil
½ tsp mustard seeds
1 medium-sized onion, chopped
1 green chilli, cut fine
1 sprig curry leaves

METHOD

1. Peel and cut tapioca into pieces.
2. Boil tapioca in salt water.
3. When half cooked, drain the water.
4. Heat oil in a pan. Deep-fry tapioca pieces. When golden remove from oil.
5. Add chilli powder. Mix well and allow to cool.
6. In another pan, heat ghee or cooking oil.

7. Fry mustard seeds, chopped onion, green chillies and curry leaves.
8. Add fried tapioca pieces. Stir and mix well.
9. Remove from stove.

Cutlets

Unlike the Western cutlet—meaning a chop or thick piece of meat, or even of fish—the Tamil cutlet is a savoury mixture of meat, fish or vegetables, ground or mashed, formed into flattened balls and deep fried. Sometimes they are coated with egg and breadcrumbs and then fried. Cutlets are eaten as an accompaniment to a rice meal or on their own as savouries.

Plantain Flower Cutlet

Vaalappu Cutlet

1 ash plantain flower, chopped fine
2 cups water
10 small onions, chopped small
3 green chillies, chopped fine
5–7 mint leaves, chopped fine
1 sprig curry leaves, chopped fine
3 tsp salt
2 tsp ground pepper
2 tbsp plain flour
3 large potatoes, boiled and mashed
1 egg
Breadcrumbs
Oil for frying

METHOD
1. Pour boiling water over plantain flower and squeeze dry.
2. Boil the flower in 2 cups water and a teaspoon of salt to remove any remaining bitterness. Strain.
3. Pound the flower or mince in a food processor.
4. Put the pounded flower in a bowl. Add onions, green chillies, mint leaves, curry leaves, salt, pepper, flour and mashed potatoes.

5. Lightly beat the egg.
6. Form small balls of the flower mixture, and flatten with fingers.
7. Coat with egg and roll in breadcrumbs. Deep-fry till golden.
8. Drain on absorbent paper and serve warm.

VARIATION

Other vegetables that may be used:
200 gm tender jackfruit pieces, boiled and mashed.
200 gm mixed vegetables—cauliflower, carrot, cabbage.

Potato Cutlets

Urulakkilangu Cutlet

6 potatoes, boiled, peeled and mashed
1 dessertspoon ghee or cooking oil
½ tsp mustard seeds
1 medium-sized onion, chopped fine
5 green chillies, chopped fine
½ tsp finely chopped garlic
½ tsp finely chopped or grated ginger
½ tsp fennel seed powder
6–8 curry leaves, chopped fine
½ tsp salt
½ tsp ground pepper
½ tsp chilli powder
5 dessertspoons plain flour
¼ tsp salt
Water to mix
Breadcrumbs
Oil for frying

METHOD

1. Heat ghee in a pan. Add mustard seeds. After a few seconds, add chopped onion, green chillies, garlic, ginger, fennel seed powder and curry leaves.
2. Add to mashed potatoes.
3. Add salt, ground pepper and chilli powder.
4. Mix well and form into little balls. Set aside.
5. Mix together plain flour, salt and enough water to make a light batter.

6. Dip each potato ball or cutlet into this batter. Then roll it in breadcrumbs.
7. Heat cooking oil in a pan. When hot, fry each cutlet, turning gently to cook evenly.
8. Drain on absorbent paper. Serve hot.

Vegetable Cutlets

Marakari Cutlet

2 cups chopped mixed vegetables: cauliflower, carrots, cabbage, leeks
¼ cup water
1 dessertspoon oil
½ tsp mustard seeds
1 medium-sized onion, chopped fine
2 green chillies, chopped fine
½ tsp chopped ginger
½ tsp chopped garlic
½ tsp fennel seed powder
½ tsp crushed cinnamon
5–7 curry leaves, chopped fine
1 dessertspoon Bengal gram flour or plain flour
A tiny piece asafoetida, crushed and dissolved in 1 tsp warm water
1 large potato, boiled, peeled and mashed
¼ tsp salt
¼ tsp turmeric powder
4 dessertspoons plain flour
Water
Breadcrumbs
Oil for frying

METHOD

1. Boil the mixed vegetables in water. Drain.
2. Heat oil in a pan. Fry mustard seeds, chopped onion, green chillies, ginger, garlic, fennel seed powder, crushed cinnamon and curry leaves.
3. Add flour and boiled vegetables. Mix well.
4. Add asafoetida. Mix well and remove from stove.
5. Mix mashed potatoes, salt, fried ingredients and turmeric in a bowl.
6. Make little balls and set aside.
7. Mix flour and enough water to make a watery batter.
8. Dip each ball in the batter and then roll it in breadcrumbs.
9. Heat oil in a pan. Deep-fry the balls till golden. Drain on absorbent paper.

Jackfruit Seed Cutlet

Pilaakottai Cutlet

2 cups jackfruit seeds
3 green chillies, chopped fine
2 medium-sized onions, chopped fine
1 tsp cumin powder
1 tsp ground pepper
1 tsp salt
1 tsp chilli powder
¼ tsp turmeric powder
5–8 curry leaves, chopped fine
¼ cup plain flour
½ cup coconut milk
Breadcrumbs
Oil for frying

METHOD

1. Boil jackfruit seeds. Peel and grind or mince them fine.
2. Add green chillies, onions, cumin powder, ground pepper, salt, chilli powder, turmeric and curry leaves.
3. Mix well. Add a little water if necessary.
4. Make little balls and set aside.
5. Mix plain flour with coconut milk to make a thin batter. Add a little salt.
6. Dip each jackfruit ball in batter and roll in breadcrumbs.
7. Heat oil in a pan. Deep-fry each cutlet till golden.
8. Drain on absorbent paper.

Meat, Chicken and Seafood Dishes

Mutton Pirattal
Mutton Fry
Dried Mutton Slices
Chicken Curry

Chicken Pathiya Curry
Chicken Bones Rasam
Crab Curry
Crab Varai

Crab Chambal
Shark Varai
Prawn Varai
Fried Squid

Dried Fish Chambal
Dried Prawn Savoury Chambal
Prawn and Tomato Chutney
Fish Curry

Fried Fish
Sprats Theeyal

Mutton Pirattal

Iraichi Pirattal

500 gm mutton, diced into bite-sized pieces
8 cloves garlic and thumb-sized ginger, pounded together
3 tbsp curry powder
2 tsp salt
2 tbsp oil
25 small red onions or 2 large onions, chopped
2 green chillies
1 tsp fenugreek seeds
1 sprig curry leaves
¼ cup water
2½ cups thick coconut milk
2 tsp roasted spices curry powder:

> ½ tsp fennel seeds
> small piece cinnamon
> 3 cloves
> 2 cardamom pods

    roast and grind together

juice of ½ lemon/lime

METHOD

1. Marinade meat with ginger and garlic, curry powder and salt for 15–20 minutes.
2. Heat oil and add chopped onion, green chillies, fenugreek seeds and curry leaves.
3. Cook till onions turn golden brown.
4. Add meat and stir well.
5. Add water and allow meat to cook.
6. Add coconut milk. Stir till well cooked.
7. Add ground spice curry powder, once meat is dry.

8. Stir well and remove from stove.
9. When cool add lemon or lime juice.

Mutton Fry

Iraichi Poriyal

500 gm lean mutton (or lamb)
1 tsp grated ginger
1 dessertspoon chilli powder
½ tsp turmeric powder
1 dessertspoon ghee
1 cup coconut milk
25 rose onions, sliced thin
1 tsp salt
1 tsp fennel seed powder

METHOD

1. Cut meat into small cubes. Marinade with ginger, chilli and turmeric powders.
2. Heat ghee. Add mutton.
3. Fry to seal the meat.
4. Add enough coconut milk to be just below the level of meat.
5. Mix well and cook meat till tender.
6. Add sliced onions and salt.
7. Turn over continuously. As coconut milk turns to oil, onions will cook in it.
8. After all the liquid is absorbed, fry till oil oozes out.
9. Add fennel seed powder. Mix well and remove.

VARIATION

Follow steps 1–7. Then deep-fry meat pieces for a crisper finish.

Dried Mutton Slices

Iraichi Vaththal

500 gm lean mutton (or lamb)
2 cups water
1 tsp turmeric powder
2 tsp cumin seeds
1 tsp fennel seeds

1 tsp peppercorns
10 cloves garlic
2 tsp salt
4 dried red chillies, pounded fine

METHOD

1. Slice meat thin.
2. Dissolve turmeric in water. Soak meat slices in water for an hour or two.
3. Drain and dry thoroughly on both sides with a cloth.
4. Roast and grind cumin, fennel seeds and peppercorns.
5. Add garlic and grind fine.
6. Add salt and grind to blend all ingredients.
7. Mix meat with dried chillies and ground ingredients.
8. Set aside in an earthen pot or glass container for a day or two.
9. Drain meat slices. Place on an aluminium tray and put out in the sun to dry.
10. In the evening return slices to the container.
11. Next day, drain the slices again and dry in the sun. Repeat process for four or five days.
12. Turn the slices over periodically for even drying. When thoroughly dry and shrivelled, remove. When cool, store till required.
13. Use in dry or wet curries.

Chicken Curry

Kodzhi Kari

500 gm boneless pieces of chicken
2 green chillies
6 cloves garlic
thumb-sized piece of fresh ginger
1 tbsp oil
2 medium-sized onions, sliced
½ tsp fenugreek seeds
1 sprig curry leaves
¼ cup water
1½ tsp salt (or to taste)
2–3 tbsp curry powder
½ cup coconut milk
1 tsp mixed aromatic spices (fennel seeds, cardamom pods, cinnamon, cloves) roasted and ground together
1½ tbsp lime/lemon juice

METHOD

1. Pound together green chillies, garlic and ginger.
2. Heat oil in a pan. Gently fry half the sliced onions, pounded mixture and fenugreek seeds. Add curry leaves.
3. Add chicken pieces.
4. Add water and salt. Cover and cook over medium flame.
5. Add curry powder. Mix well together and continue to cook, uncovered.
6. Add remaining onions and coconut milk, stirring constantly to avoid burning.
7. When well cooked, remove from stove and add mixed aromatic spices. Sprinkle lime/lemon juice.

Chicken Pathiya Curry

Pathiya Kari

Like the vegetarian Charakku Kari, Pathiya Curry is a preparation given to lactating mothers.

200 gm young chicken, cut into bite-sized pieces
3½ tsp coriander seeds
½ tsp cumin seeds
½ tsp pepper
1 dried red chilli
10 small onions or 1 large onion, chopped
¼ tsp fenugreek seeds
a pinch turmeric powder
6 cloves garlic
salt to taste
2 cups water
½ tsp tamarind pulp
6–8 curry leaves
1 tbsp thick coconut milk

METHOD

1. Grind fine together coriander seeds, cumin seeds, pepper and dried chilli.
2. Fill a pan with 1½ cups water. Toss in chicken pieces. Cover and cook onions, fenugreek seeds, turmeric, garlic and salt.
3. Mix ground ingredients and tamarind in half cup water.
4. Add to pan, together with curry leaves and coconut milk.
5. Bring to boil. Simmer for two minutes and turn off flame.

Idi-appam (p. 2)

Puttu (p. 4)

Aalanggai Puttu (p. 6)

Appam (floppers) (p. 14)

Palmyra Fruit (p. 96)

(Top) Pidi Kolukattai (p. 115), *(Centre)* Mothagam (p. 114) and
(Bottom) Kolukattai (p. 113)

Murukku (p. 116)

Murukku Maker (p. 116)

Puttu and Murukku Makers

Chicken Bone Rasam

Kodzhi Elumbu Rasam

½ kg chicken bones, roughly chopped into small pieces
2 tbsp coriander seeds ⎫
1 tsp peppercorns   ⎬ grind together
1 tsp cumin seeds   ⎭
3 cups water
1 onion, chopped
2 green chillies
1 tomato, chopped
2 tbsp coconut milk (optional)
8 cloves garlic, pounded roughly
1 tsp lime/lemon juice

METHOD

1. Tie ground ingredients into a little bundle in a piece of fine cotton cloth.
2. Put all the ingredients in a pan.
3. Add coconut milk if desired.
4. When the ingredients have boiled through (about 20 minutes), remove from stove. Add lime/lemon juice.
5. Strain liquid from the pan and serve in a bowl as accompaniment to a rice meal.

VARIATION

The rasam can be changed into a soup by adding 1 cup of firm vegetables, cubed.

Crab Curry

Nandu Curry

500 gm crabs, cleaned
10 small onions or 1 large onion
2 green chillies
½ tsp fenugreek seeds
6 cloves garlic and thumb-size ginger, ground to a paste
1 tsp salt
2 ½ tbsp curry powder
1 cup coconut milk
2 tbsp shredded coconut

1 sprig curry leaves
1 tsp fennel seed powder
juice of ½ lemon/lime

METHOD

1. In a pan, place crabs, chopped onions, green chillies, fenugreek seeds, ground ginger-garlic, salt, curry powder and coconut milk. Mix well together and cook.
2. Once crabs are cooked, add shredded coconut, curry leaves and fennel seed powder.
3. Simmer over low flame. Stir ingredients constantly till gravy is thick.
4. Remove from stove.
5. Add lime/lemon juice.

Note: Prawns and squid (cuttlefish) can be cooked in the same way.

Crab Varai

Nandu Varai

3–4 crabs
½ dessertspoon curry powder
¼ tsp turmeric powder
1 cup grated coconut
2 tsp oil
1 medium-sized onion, chopped fine
½ tsp mustard seeds
½ tsp fennel seeds
3 dried red chillies, cut fine
1 sprig curry leaves
½ tsp salt
1½ tsp lime/lemon juice

METHOD

1. Boil crabs. Scrape all flesh (from body, legs and pincers).
2. Mix together crab flesh, curry powder, turmeric and grated coconut.
3. Heat oil. Sauté chopped onion, mustard seeds, fennel seeds, dried chillies and curry leaves.
4. Add crab-flesh mixture and salt. Toss together.
5. When well mixed, add lime or lemon juice and remove from stove.

Crab Chambal

Nandu Chambal

3–4 crabs
2 dessertspoons grated coconut
1 small onion, chopped and crushed lightly
6–8 curry leaves, crushed lightly
½ tsp salt
1½ tsp lime/lemon juice

METHOD

1. Roast crabs in hot embers or boil in water.
2. Remove flesh, in chunks as large as possible.
3. Mix all the ingredients together.

Shark Varai

Churaa Varai

250 gm shark flesh (flake)
1 cup grated coconut
¼ tsp turmeric powder
½ tsp pepper powder
1 tsp cumin seed powder
1 tsp salt
¼ tsp chilli powder (if desired hot)
1½ tbsp oil
10 small onions or 1 large onion, chopped
4 dried red chillies
½ tsp mustard seeds
1 sprig curry leaves

METHOD

1. Steam or poach the shark flesh.
2. When cool, shred it. Add grated coconut, turmeric, pepper, cumin, salt and chilli powder (optional).
3. Mix together well.
4. Heat oil in a wok. Add onions. Fry till transparent.
5. Add dried chillies, mustard seeds and curry leaves. Fry till mustard seeds pop.
6. Add the shark flesh mixture and toss over low flame till well blended.

The shark that is cooked in Tamil dishes is the 'Paal Chura' or 'Milk Shark', a small and light ash-coloured variety. Where Paal Chura is not available, Flake can be substituted quite effectively.

Prawn Varai

Raal Varai

1. Substitute 500 gm cleaned and deveined prawns for the shark in the recipe earlier.
2. Boil prawns in a little water till well cooked.
3. Pound or shred them in a food processor.
4. Proceed as for Shark Varai (p. 77).

Fried Squid

Kanavaai Poriyal

500 gm squid, cleaned and sliced
6 cloves garlic, pounded
½ inch ginger, pounded
¼ tsp turmeric powder
2 tsp chilli powder
2 dessertspoons oil
3 green chillies, chopped
1 sprig curry leaves
1 medium-sized onion, chopped or 8 rose onions, sliced
½ tsp salt

METHOD

1. Marinade pieces of squid with garlic, ginger, turmeric and chilli powder. Set aside for at least half an hour.
2. Heat oil. Add pieces of squid. Cover and cook.
3. When almost cooked, add green chillies, curry leaves, onions and salt. Cook uncovered.
4. Stir continuously to avoid burning and until gravy is almost dry.
5. Remove from flame.

Dried Fish Chambal

Karuvaattu Chambal

1 large piece salted and dried fish
2 green chillies, chopped
2 big onions, chopped
4–6 curry leaves, chopped fine

1 tbsp   dried red chillies, crushed
2 dessertspoons   tamarind pulp
½ cup   coconut milk
¼ tsp   salt

METHOD

1. Roast salted and dried fish over stove. Allow to cool a little and break into small pieces.
2. Add green chillies, onions, curry leaves and crushed red chillies.
3. Add tamarind pulp and coconut milk.
4. Add salt. Mix well together using hands.
5. Serve with Puttu or String Hoppers.

Dried Prawn Savoury Chambal

Vettai Thanni

Vettai Thanni literally means 'Hunter's Water'. This is a quick preparation, made for a traveller or, in the past, for a hunter to take away to be eaten with plain rice. Eaten with rice and a little water makes it a complete meal.

1 cup   dried prawns, roasted slightly
½ cup   chopped onions
2   green chillies, chopped
5–7   curry leaves
1 dessertspoon   grated mango or 2 tsp tamarind pulp
Salt to taste

METHOD

1. Pound or grind all the ingredients together.
2. Ensure it is not ground fine enough to form a paste.
3. Can be stored for a few days.

Prawn and Tomato Chutney

Raal Thakkali Chutney

250 gm   prawns, shelled and de-veined
2   tomatoes, skinned
1 dessertspoon   oil
½ tsp   mustard seeds

¼ tsp fennel seeds
5–8 curry leaves, chopped fine
Thumb-sized ginger, cut into thin strips about an inch long
2–3 dried red chillies, soaked and ground or 1 tsp chilli powder

METHOD

1. Blanch and peel tomatoes.
2. Mash and set them aside.
3. Heat oil. Splutter mustard and fennel seeds in it.
4. Add curry leaves, ginger and ground chilli.
5. Add prawns and toss to coat completely.
6. Add a little water. Allow prawns to cook.
7. Add tomatoes and salt.
8. Allow chutney to thicken and remove from stove.

Fish Curry

Meen Kari

1 kg fish (any firm variety), cut into slices
2 cups water
1 onion, chopped
2 green chillies, chopped
½ tsp turmeric powder
1 tsp thick tamarind pulp
1½ tsp salt
2 dessertspoons curry powder
2 tsp cumin seeds
1 tsp pepper
8 cloves garlic
½ cup coconut milk
1½ tsp fenugreek seeds
1 sprig curry leaves, chopped
(Rub a tsp turmeric and juice of half a lime/
lemon on the fish. Wash away before cooking.
This gets rid of the "fishy" smell.)

METHOD

1. Mix the chopped onions, green chillies, turmeric, tamarind pulp, salt and curry powder. Boil together.
2. Add fish slices.

3. Grind cumin seeds and pepper. Crush garlic with ground cumin and pepper.
4. Mix ground ingredients in coconut milk.
5. Add to the pan. Add fenugreek seeds.
6. Cook till it boils. Lower flame and simmer for two minutes.
7. Add curry leaves and remove from flame.

Note: Do not cover at once. Allow it to cool a little before covering.

Fried Fish

Meen Poriyal

6 slices medium-to-large sized fish
   (trevally, mackeral, cod, salmon, pomfret, etc may be used.)
2 tsp grated ginger
4 cloves garlic
1 tsp chilli powder
½ tsp turmeric powder
½ tsp salt
1 tsp lime/lemon juice
Oil for frying

METHOD
1. Pound ginger and garlic.
2. Mix together with chilli powder, turmeric, salt and lime or lemon juice.
3. Marinade fish in this paste. Set aside for at least half an hour.
4. In a shallow frying pan, heat oil.
5. Shallow-fry fish, turning each piece carefully to cook on both sides.
6. Drain on absorbent paper.

Note: A little cumin seed powder or Charakku curry powder may be added to the marinade. It will enhance the flavour though it may darken the fish on frying.

Sprats Theeyal

Nethali Meen Theeyal

250 gm sprats, cleaned and washed or dried sprats
7 dried red chillies, crushed and pounded
1 mature green mango or 3 pieces dried mango or
1 dessertspoon tamarind pulp

1 medium onion, chopped
½ tsp salt (to taste if using dried sprats)
6 cloves garlic, crushed
1 sprig curry leaves
Water as required

METHOD

1. Arrange sprats in a pot, in layers if necessary.
2. Add pounded dried chillies.
3. Add mango or tamarind pulp, chopped onion, salt and garlic.
4. Add water to almost cover (¾ way up) sprats.
5. Cook on medium flame. When liquid is almost absorbed, add curry leaves.
6. Remove from flame.

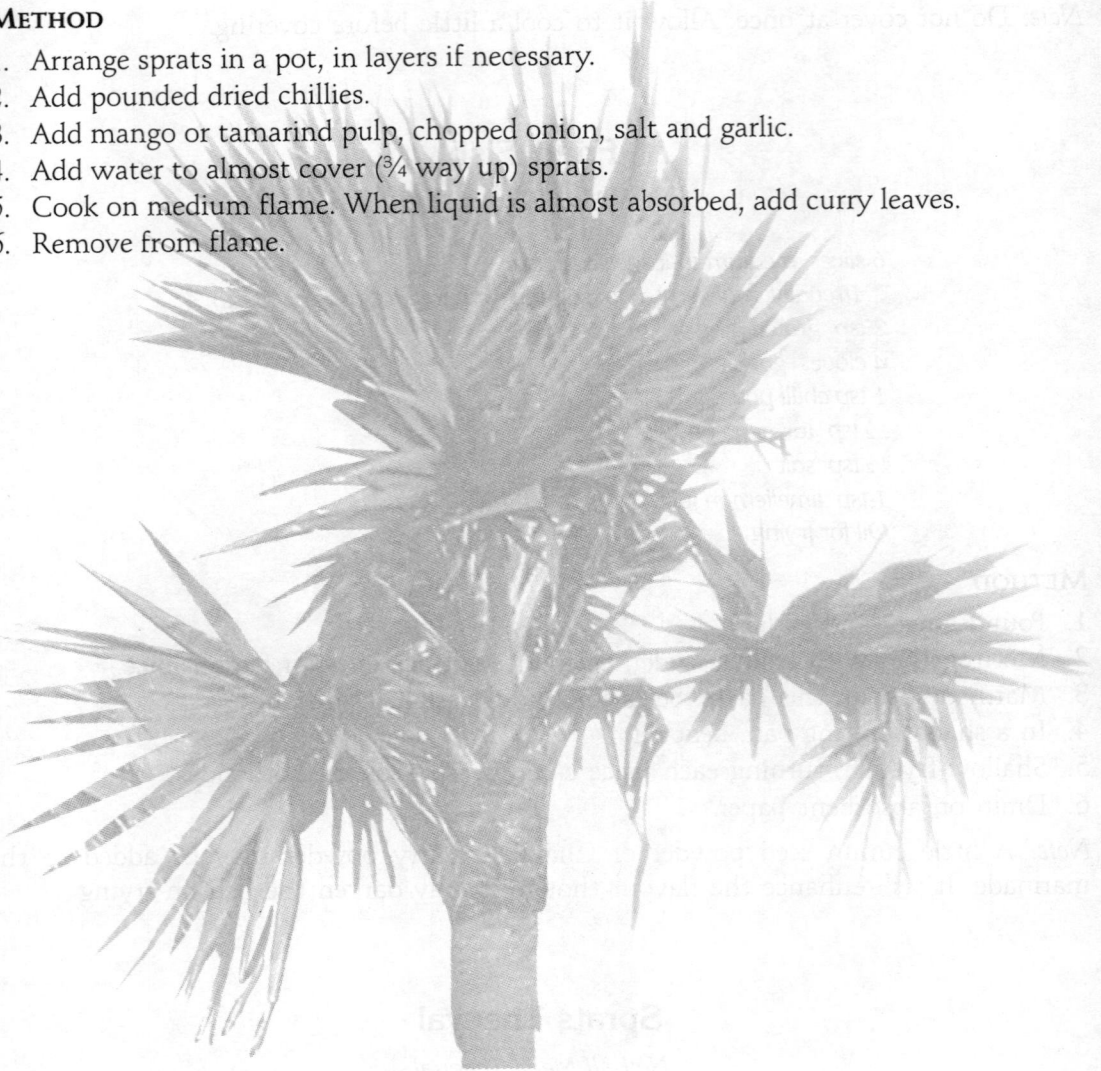

Achars, Pickles and Vadahams

Mixed Vegetable Achar
Long Bean Achar
Bitter Gourd Achar
Aubergine/Brinjal Achar

Jackfruit Seed Achar
Date Achar
Kadambam Achar
Lime Pickle

Mango Pickle
Bitter Gourd Vadaham
Margossa Flower Vadaham
Rice Vadaham

Rice Flakes Vadaham
Buttermilk Chillies
Dried Mango Slices

Achar

Achar (or Acharu as it is locally known) is not strictly an 'authentic' Jaffna preparation. In cross-cultural relations with neighbouring communities—the Malays, the Muslims from other parts of South Asia and the Sinhalese—achars have become a part of Tamil cuisine. They have the advantage of tasting better after a few days and so can be made and stored. Their sweet-sour-hot flavour makes them popular. The Tamils have adopted achars as their own and given them a distinct identity in flavour.

Mixed Vegetable Achar

Kalantha Marakkari Acharu

1   thumb-sized piece ginger
5 cloves garlic
4 cloves
1 small piece cinnamon
½ tsp chilli powder
1 tbsp lime/lemon juice
½ cup onions, cut lengthways
½ cup capsicum, sliced and cut into 1-inch lengths
½ cup pineapple cut into small pieces
½ cup pitted dates
1 tsp powdered mustard
1 tsp salt
1 tsp sugar
¼ cup white vinegar

METHOD

1. Pound ginger and garlic together.
2. In a bowl (not brass or aluminium) mix together cloves, cinnamon, chilli powder, lime/lemon juice and the pounded ginger-garlic.

3. Add all the vegetables. Mix well together.
4. Add mustard powder, salt and sugar.
5. Put mixture into a bottle. Pour vinegar over the vegetables.
6. Leave to mature for about three or four days.

Long Bean Achar

Paithanggaai Acharu

200 gm long beans cut into 1-inch lengths
Oil for frying
6–7 cloves garlic, whole
6 green chillies, seeded and sliced
1 medium-sized onion, chopped fine
3 tbsp vinegar
½ tsp salt
1½ tsp chilli powder
1½ tsp sugar
6–8 curry leaves

METHOD

1. Heat oil in a pan. Fry long beans and drain oil into a bowl.
2. Fry garlic, green chillies and onion. Drain and add to long beans.
3. Put vinegar, salt, chilli powder, sugar and curry leaves in a pot (not brass or aluminium).
4. Bring to boil.
5. Add the long beans and mix thoroughly.
6. As soon as it reaches boiling point, remove and allow to cool.
7. Store in sterilised bottles and leave to mature for a few days.

Bitter Gourd Achar

Paavakkaai Acharu

2 cups bitter gourd, seeded and chopped into 1-inch lengths
6 cloves garlic
2 tsp mustard seeds

1 thumb-sized piece ginger
6 dried red chillies
¾ cup vinegar
1 tsp salt
2 tsp sugar

METHOD

1. Grind garlic, mustard seeds, ginger and dried chillies to a paste. Add vinegar if necessary to make grinding easier.
2. Boil vinegar and a little salt. Remove and allow to cool.
3. Add ground ingredients and bitter gourd, salt and sugar. Mix thoroughly.
4. When really cool store in sterilised bottles. Will keep up to a week.

Aubergine/Brinjal Achar

Kaththarikkaai Acharu

200 gm aubergine (brinjal) cut into inch-long pieces
A pinch turmeric powder
Oil for frying
5 green chillies, chopped
2 medium-sized onions, chopped
1 tsp crushed mustard seeds (or mustard powder)
½ tsp salt
2 tsp sugar
1½ tsp chilli powder
¾ cup vinegar

METHOD

1. Rub pieces of brinjal with turmeric. Allow to stand for a few minutes.
2. Heat oil and deep-fry pieces of brinjal till brown. Drain and place on absorbent paper.
3. Deep-fry green chillies and chopped onions. Drain and add to brinjal.
4. In a pot (not brass or aluminium) put in crushed mustard seeds, salt, sugar, chilli powder and vinegar. Mix well.
5. Add the fried brinjal, green chillies and onions. Mix well with a wooden spoon.
6. When cool, store in sterilised bottles.

Jackfruit Seeds Achar

Pilaakottai Acharu

200 gm jackfruit seeds (young seeds before the flesh of the fruit ripens round it)
¾ cup vinegar
½ cup water
4 dried red chillies
½ tsp ground pepper
4 cloves garlic
thumb-sized piece ginger
2 tsp mustard seeds
1 tsp sugar
salt to taste

METHOD

1. Clean and skin jackfruit seeds. Halve and de-vein. Chop into quarters.
2. In a pot (not brass or aluminium) bring vinegar and water to boil. Add jackfruit seeds and cook till tender.
3. Grind dried chillies, pepper, garlic, ginger and mustard seeds to a paste, adding vinegar if necessary.
4. Separately grind jackfruit seeds, sugar and salt. Mixture should be dry.
5. Mix all the ingredients together.
6. Spread on a shallow tray.
7. Cut the pieces as required.
8. Transfer to a bowl or glass jar and refrigerate. Will keep for a week or so.

Date Achar

Perichampala Acharu

200 gm dates, pitted and halved
¾ cup vinegar
a small piece cinnamon
6 cloves
¾ tsp salt
½ tsp ground pepper

METHOD

1. Place dates in a sterilised bottle.
2. In a pan (not brass or aluminium) bring to boil, vinegar, cinnamon, cloves, salt and pepper.
3. Remove and pour into bottle of dates.
4. Allow to cool. Close and shake bottle to distribute liquid evenly.
5. Allow to mature for 7 or 8 days.

VARIATION

Bombay onions, beetroot and green chillies can be used in the same way. If used, 2 teaspoons of sugar may be added to the boiling vinegar mixture.

'Kadambam' Achar

'Kadambam' is a colloquial term meaning mixed.

4 cloves garlic
1 slice ginger
½ cup pitted dates
½ cup small rose onions, quartered
½ cup capsicum, cut into pieces
½ cup unripe mangoes, cut into small pieces
½ cup pineapple pieces
6 cloves
1 tsp mustard powder (or crushed mustard seeds)
½ tsp chilli powder
1 tsp sugar
1 tsp salt
1 dessertspoon lime/lemon juice
¼ cup vinegar

METHOD

1. Crush garlic and ginger.
2. Cut the dates into quarters.
3. Mix all the ingredients. Set aside.
4. Stir the pickle a couple of times. Store in a sterilised bottle.
5. Shake the bottle every now and then.
6. Allow to mature for a day or two. Will keep for more than a week if refrigerated.

Lime Pickle

Uruggaai

10 limes
¼ cup salt
juice of 10 limes
¼ cup water
1 tsp fenugreek seeds
¼ tsp asafoetida powder or a tiny piece of asafoetida soaked in a tsp of warm water
½ tsp turmeric powder
2 dessertspoons gingelly oil
1 tsp mustard seeds
2 dried red chillies, pounded or ½ tsp chilli powder

METHOD

1. Score each of the 10 limes into four (without cutting them completely).
2. Pack each with salt.
3. Arrange in a wide-mouthed dish or a jar, with cut sides facing up.
4. Set aside for 3–5 days for limes to soak in salt.
5. Put jar out in the sun, till limes dry and shrivel slightly.
6. At this stage, they are ready to be seasoned and pickled.
7. In a container, mix the juice of 10 limes and water.
8. Roast fenugreek seeds and asafoetida for a minute in a dry pan. Remove and grind together. Add to lime juice.
9. Add turmeric to lime juice.
10. In a pan, heat gingelly oil and fry mustard seeds till they pop.
11. Add crushed chilli or chilli powder.
12. Add the lime juice mixture. Mix together and remove pan. Allow to cool a little.
13. Dip each dried lime in it and arrange in a jar.
14. Pour the remaining liquid over the limes.
15. Cover jar with lid and allow limes to soak. This pickle keeps very well.

Mango Pickle

Maanggaai Uruggaai

3 green mangoes cut into small pieces
½ tsp fenugreek seeds
¼ tsp asafoetida powder or a tiny piece of crushed asafoetida

1½ dessertspoons coconut oil
½ tsp mustard seeds
1½ tsp salt
1 tsp chilli powder
¼ tsp turmeric powder

METHOD

1. Roast fenugreek seeds and asafoetida in a dry pan and grind together.
2. Heat oil in a pan. Add mustard seeds and fry till they pop.
3. Add mango pieces, salt and ground spices.
4. Cover and cook for a few minutes.
5. Uncover and add chilli and turmeric powder. Stir and mix well.
6. Store in a sterilised bottle till required.

Vadaham

One of the ways of preserving fruit, vegetables or flowers in season for later use, is by making Vadahams. These are spicy preparations that are dried in the sun and stored in airtight containers till needed. They are then deep-fried as required. They can be stored indefinitely if kept in airtight containers.

Bitter Gourd Vadaham

Paavakkaai Vadaham

¾ cup split black gram (urad dal)
¾ cup bitter gourd, grated coarsely
5–6 green chillies, chopped fine
2 dessertspoons onions, chopped fine
2 tsp chilli powder
¼ tsp fennel seed powder
¼ tsp turmeric powder
1½ tsp salt

METHOD

1. Soak the black gram for two hours. Grind coarsely.
2. Mix all the other ingredients with ground gram.
3. Form into little balls and then flatten each.
4. Lay a white cloth (a saree or veshti is normally used) on a large tray.

5. Lay vadahams on cloth to sun-dry for a few days, till completely dry.
6. Remove from cloth. Dry cloth and place vadahams on it again for a thorough drying.
7. When dry remove and store the vadahams.
8. Fry as needed.

Margossa Flower Vadaham

Vepampuu Vadaham

The margossa or neem tree is well documented for its medicinal value. Almost all parts of the tree are used—the leaves and flowers in cooking, the twigs are crushed at one end to make effective 'toothbrushes', and the oil has almost miraculous healing properties. A bunch of margossa leaves is often tied together to make a 'scratching brush' to ease the itchiness resulting at the end of an attack of measles or chicken pox. Most people in South India and the Tamil homelands try to have a margossa tree in their yard, if they can, to ward off illnesses.

1 cup split black gram (urad dal)
3 cups margossa flowers, cleaned, without twigs
2 tsp fennel seeds
1 tsp peppercorns
1 tsp cumin seeds
2 tsp salt
10 green chillies, chopped fine
½ cup onion, chopped
2 dessertspoons garlic, chopped
2–3 tsp chilli powder
¼ cup sesame seeds
1 sprig curry leaves, chopped fine

METHOD

1. Soak black gram. Grind coarsely and set aside.
2. Roast fennel seeds, peppercorns and cumin seeds.
3. Add to ground black gram.
4. Add margossa flowers and salt.
5. Mix all the ingredients together.
6. Form vadahams by making small balls from the mixture. Flatten each.
7. Sun-dry on a white cloth for 4–5 days.
8. Store till needed.
9. These should be deep-fried when required.

Rice Vadaham

Arisi Vadaham

2 cups white long grained rice
25 green chillies
A tiny piece asafoetida
½ cup sago
2 cups buttermilk
4 cups water
½ dessertspoon salt
2 dessertspoons lime juice

METHOD

1. Soak the rice for an hour. Grind.
2. Dry the flour in the sun.
3. Grind green chillies and asafoetida together.
4. In a pan put sago, buttermilk and water. Cook together.
5. When sago is well-cooked (transparent), add the ground rice flour.
6. Stir well to avoid lumps forming.
7. Lower the flame. Close with a lid and simmer for a few minutes.
8. Turn off the flame and remove. Allow to cool.
9. Add salt, ground chillies and lime juice. Mix well.
10. Soak a large piece of white cloth in water. Wring it dry and lay it on a large tray.
11. Fill a murukku mould with the mixture. Form strips straight on to the white cloth. Cut into strips about 1–2 inches long with a butter knife.
12. Set tray out in the sun for a day or two. Remove strips from cloth and put them on a tray.
13. Set out in the sun to dry out completely.
14. Store in an airtight bottle till required.
15. Deep-fry when required.

Rice Flakes Vadaham

Aval Vadaham

4 cups rice flakes (aval)
½ cup sago
20 green chillies
A tiny piece asafoetida
100 gm young okra

3 tsp salt
2 dessertspoons yoghurt
4 tsp lime juice
1½ dessertspoons white poppy seeds
2 cups water

METHOD

1. Boil sago in water till almost completely dissolved.
2. Remove and set aside to cool.
3. Grind together green chillies and asafoetida.
4. Chop okra into fine pieces.
5. Add rice flakes and okra to sago liquid.
6. Add ground chillies, salt, yoghurt, lime juice and poppy seeds.
7. Mix well.
8. Soak a large piece of white cloth in water. Wring it dry and lay it on a large tray.
9. Make lime-sized balls of rice-flake mixture and flatten very thin on to the cloth in the tray.
10. Sun-dry the rice flake vadahams for a couple of days.
11. Later remove the vadahams from the cloth (sprinkle water on the back of the cloth if necessary). Place them on a tray and dry them again, making sure to turn them on both sides.
12. When completely dry, store and deep-fry when required.

Buttermilk Chillies

Mor Milaggaai

500 gm tender green chillies
5 cups sour yoghurt
6 tsp salt

METHOD

1. In an earthen or glass container, soak green chillies in yoghurt and salt. (To increase absorption of yoghurt, chillies may be slit at the bottom end, but this is not absolutely necessary.)
2. Cover and set aside for 5–6 days. Stir every day.
3. Put the container out in the sun for a further 3–4 days.
4. Drain chillies each morning and sun-dry them on a large tray. At night put chillies back into yoghurt. Repeat this process until all the yoghurt has been absorbed.

5. Sun-dry chillies for a further 3–4 days.
6. Store till ready to use. Deep-fry as required.

Note: The older the chillies, the hotter they will be.

Dried Mango Slices
Maanggaai Vaththal

5 mature green mangoes
¼ cup salt

METHOD
1. Cut mangoes and remove seeds. Slice lengthways, into 8 slices.
2. Mix with salt.
3. Leave to soak in an earthen or glass container for two days.
4. On the third day, shake off salt and put mango slices out to dry.
5. At night return them to the container with salt. Repeat this process for 4 or 5 days.
6. Finally, sun-dry mango slices till shrivelled.
7. Use as required in fish curry, sothi or other curries.

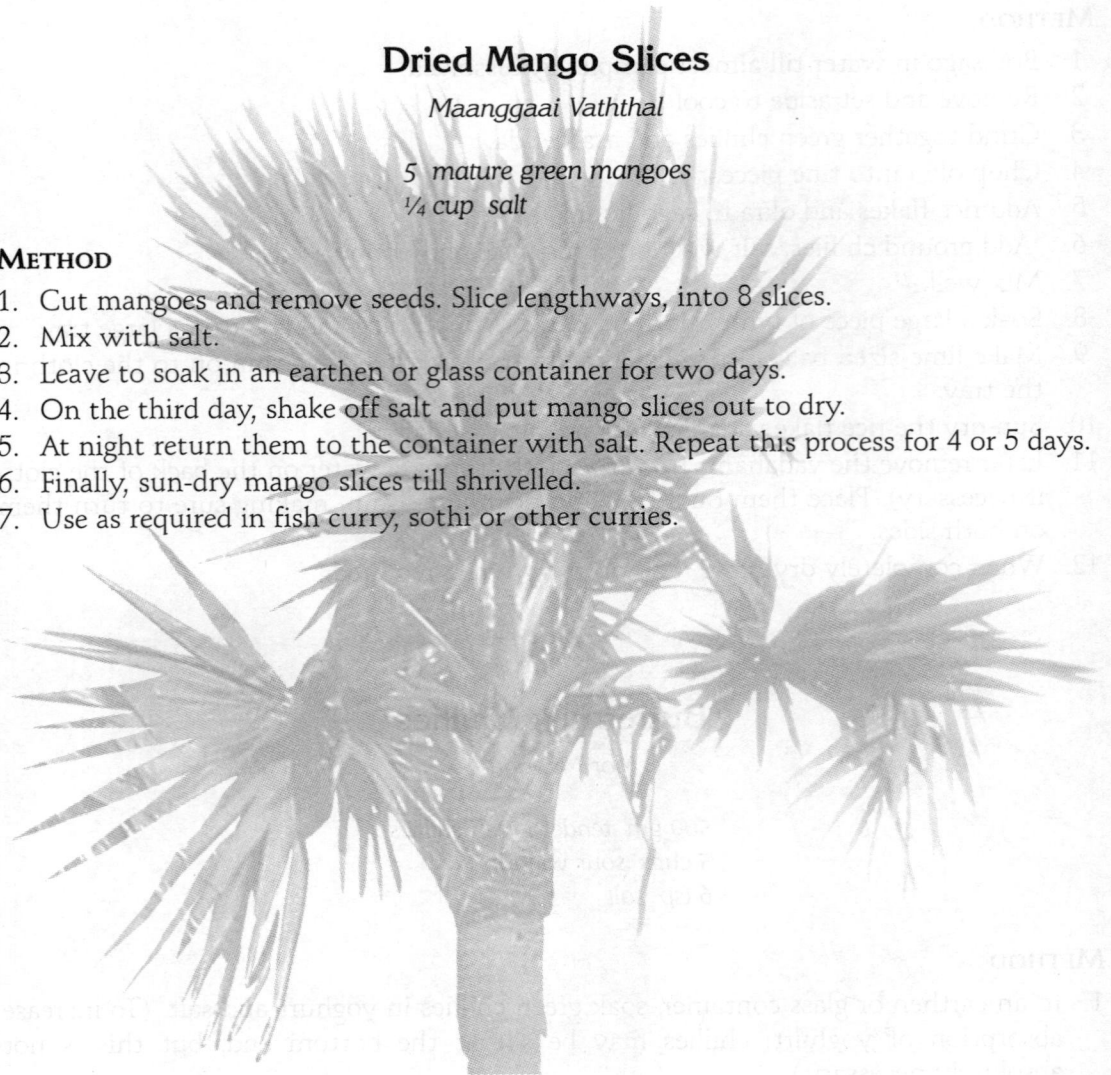

Gifts of the Palmyra Palm

Palmyra Root
Karupani Kool
Palmyra Root Flour Puttu
Spinach Odiyal Puttu

Sprats (Nethali) Odiyal Puttu
Dried Prawn Odiyal Puttu
Palmyra Fruit Drink
Pananggaai Paniyaaram

Pinaatu
Paani Pinaatu
Odiyal Dosa
Panangkilangu Thuvayal

Pulukkodiyal Laddu
Savoury Pulukkodiyal Balls
Pulukkodiyal-Semolina Laddu
Pulukkodiyal Vadai

Palmyra Plup Thosai
Palmyra Fruit Payasam
Vattalappam
Pulukkodiyal Alwa

Pulukkodiyal Flour Cookies
Palmyra Fruit Dodol
Palmyra Fruit Cake
Pulukkodiyal Flour Butter Cake

The Palmyra Palm

Borassus Flabellifer

The Jaffna Peninsula and the islands to the north are the home of the tall, sturdy palmyra palm, the *panamaram*. From its crown of fan-shaped leaves to its roots, this palm serves the Tamil people. It is an intrinsic part of the life and cuisine of Tamils in the North and East—so much so that the Tamils identify with it totally, and, wherever nicknames spell happy jousting, the Jaffna Tamil is referred to as a 'panang-kottai' or palmyra seed.

It is the single most useful plant in the region. The leaves are dried and used to thatch roofs and for fencing. Mats, fans, baskets, nesting boxes and winnowing fans, baby's rattles and door hangings and many other items of both decorative and functional value emerge from the deft hands of women, weaving strips of the leaves.

The flowers from the male tree yield the sweet 'karupani'—surely the nectar of the gods! *"We would wait for the 'Karupani' nachiyar. Our trees were farmed to a family that tapped the karupani. They gave us an earthen jar of it and kept the rest. I was not too sure of the mercantile arrangements of it all—I only waited for the jar of karupani."* Rani Thangarajah's eyes glisten with the joyful memories of a Jaffna childhood.

"In the sun I can still picture her statuesque form, walking with her straight back and steady pace, as she crossed from the edge of our yard towards the house. On the tiruggani [circular ring placed on the head] her earthenware pot balanced, the light cotton saree drawn across her naked breasts. She was a very beautiful woman. She would place the pot on the ground on our verendah. I would run eagerly towards it. I would put my face towards its mouth just to drink in the aroma! Mother would shoo me away. But as soon as she had given Karupani Chellamah a drink and some old saree or other for her pains, she would let me enjoy the full joy of the karupani." She gave a delighted laugh and I could see the other women partaking in her remembered ecstasy.

"Amma would have got the mangoes ready. They would be cut into the tiniest of pieces. We each got our homely bowl of karupani, and the mango thundus (pieces) would be put in. With unadulterated bliss we would raise the heavenly bowl to our lips and drink. This was both the nectar and ambrosia of the gods!"

Karupani would thus be used as itself. It would also be boiled to make jaggery. It is fermented to make toddy, an intoxicating drink. As the female tree's flowers do not produce too sweet a nectar, they are not tapped but allowed to be pollinated by bees and other insects with pollen from the male tree flowers. They then form the palmyra fruit.

The fruit contains a colourless jelly-like substance called 'nongu'—delicious to eat. It also contains three seeds. These seeds are put into specially prepared nurseries. After three or three-and-a-half months, thick roots are formed. The seeds are gently lifted out of the soil and the roots broken off. Their sheath of skin is removed. They are either dried as they are and become 'odiyal', or are boiled and dried to form 'pulukkodiyal', which is often cut into slices and becomes a nutritious snack for long-distance travellers and pilgrims.

The trunks are cut down for timber for building. In the long-drawn out civil war in the North and East, they have been used to build bunkers and shelters. Thus millions of trees have been felled and the reforestation of palmyra palms is an urgent concern.

The palmyra palm is very much a part of the culinary–cultural psyche of the Tamils in the North and East of the island.

Palmyra Root

Odiyal Kool

1 cup palmyra root (odiyal) flour
1 tbsp uncooked rice
1½ l water
1 cup long beans, cut into about 2 cm pieces
1 cup tapioca, cubed
5 pieces ripe jackfruit pulp
10 jackfruit seeds
1 whole young crab, shelled and cleaned
10 medium-sized prawns
10 small pieces fish or a fish-head
½ tsp turmeric powder
1 cup drumstick (murunggaai) leaves
15 dried red chillies (ground to a paste)
1 tsp tamarind pulp

METHOD

1. Soak palmyra flour in water.
2. Cook rice in water.

3. When cooked, add long beans, tapioca, jackfruit pulp and jackfruit seeds.
4. After about 5 minutes, add seafood, turmeric powder and drumstick leaves.
5. Reduce flame and simmer.
6. Meanwhile, drain the palmyra flour. Add fresh water and drain again. Repeat the process to eliminate the bitterness from the flour.
7. Add chilli paste to the drained flour and mix well. Add mixture to the pan. Add tamarind pulp and stir mixture gently till all the ingredients are cooked.
8. Remove from stove and serve hot.

Kanthapilla Velupillai, popularly known as "Kallady" Velupillai, the poet, is a well-known figure in Jaffna Tamil literature. Once, travelling far from his village of Vasavilan, he went through Ratnapura to the house of his friend, Suppiah, in Nivityagola. He was exhausted by the time he got there.

Suppiah's wife made some Odiyal Kool, knowing how fond the poet was of it. Adding banana chips to the Kool, she served it in a dish and set it between the two friends.

Folding the jackfruit tree leaves into a cone and securing it with a piece of coconut leaf spine-stick (iikul-kuchi) the two friends scooped the Kool and relished it in ecstasy. At the end of the meal, not only was "Kallady" Veluppillai's hunger assuaged, his tiredness too seemed to have evaporated! In great appreciation he addressed Suppiah's wife and sang,

"You who wear garlands of flowers so fresh that the bees hover over them,
Coming from far-off Ratnapura to Nityagola,
'Kalladyan' relished your Kool with his friend Suppiah."

Karupani Kool

The nectar of the male palmyra palm, 'karupani' is very sweet. Sometimes green mangoes are peeled and cut into tiny pieces and simply put into the karupani and eaten. 'Heavenly, after a bath at Keerimalai!' is a remark typical of the reaction to this particular gift of the palmyra palm.

> 1½ l karupani
> 2–3 tsp cumin seeds
> ½ tsp pepper
> ¼ tsp salt
> 2–3 dessertspoons split green gram (moong dal), roasted
> ½ cup tiny slices of coconut
> 1 cup long grain rice flour, unroasted
> ½ cup coconut milk

METHOD

1. Roast cumin seeds, pepper and salt. Grind together. Set aside.
2. Strain the karupani. Add the split green gram. Boil till green gram is soft.
3. Add slices of coconut.
4. Meanwhile, mix rice flour and coconut milk into a smooth paste.
5. Add the ground spices to the coconut milk and mix well.
6. Add this mixture to the pot a little at a time, stirring all the time.
7. Bring to boil and remove at once. (The kool tends to thicken if left on the flame too long.)

Palmyra Root Flour Puttu

Odiyalmaa Puttu

1 cup palmyra root (odiyal) flour
½ cup grated coconut
2–3 green chillies, chopped very fine
1 medium-sized onion, chopped very fine
½ tsp salt
a little water
2–3 dessertspoons ghee or butter

METHOD

1. Mix palmyra root flour, grated coconut, chopped green chillies, onion and salt. Sprinkle water to form a grainy texture, rolling it between the fingers.
2. Steam in a neethu petti if possible. If not available, any puttu steamer will do.
3. When ready, turn it over into a container. Make a well in the centre. Pour the ghee or butter in it. Cover with the puttu.
4. Mix just before serving.

VARIATION

Spinach Odiyal Puttu   Finely chopped spinach may be added to puttu mixture before steaming.

Sprats Odiyal Puttu   Boil a handful of sprats (nethali meen). Shred the flesh and add to puttu mixture before steaming.

Dried Prawn Odiyal Puttu   Roast 2 dessertspoons of dried prawns. Pound lightly and add to puttu mixture before steaming.

Palmyra Fruit Drink

Panangkali Kodial

1 cup palmyra fruit pulp
1 cup sugar
3 cloves
2 cups water
Lime/lemon juice to taste

METHOD

1. Boil sugar, cloves and water.
2. Add palmyra fruit pulp. Bring to boil and allow it to simmer for about ten minutes.
3. Add 4 parts water to every one part fruit drink. Add lime/lemon juice and ice cubes, if desired.
4. If refrigerated it can keep up to a week.

Pananggaai Paniyaram

1½ cups thick palmyra fruit pulp
3 cups plain flour
1½ cups sugar
½ cup coconut milk
1 tsp baking powder
Oil for frying

METHOD

1. Steam the plain flour. Allow it to cool. Roast in a dry pan over a low flame, making sure it does not burn. Allow it to cool.
2. If pulp is fibrous, strain it.
3. Mix flour, palmyra fruit pulp, sugar, coconut milk and baking powder.
4. Heat oil in a frying pan. Drop spoonfuls of batter into the hot oil.
5. Fry till golden and drain on absorbent paper.

Pinaatu

This special palmyra toffee is an integral part of Jaffna culture. The pulp of the palmyra fruit is extracted and dried in the sun. Successive layers create a slab. Four poles are planted in the ground and a white saree or veshti is tied to the four poles, forming a platform-tray to receive the pulp to be dried. If rain is anticipated at night it is taken indoors; if not, a mat is spread over it to form a cover.

METHOD

1. Take a very ripe palmyra fruit.
2. Peel and sprinkle water over the fruit if it is not too soft. The softer the flesh the better.
3. Scrape off pulp with a spoon into a container. When the whole fruit has been scraped, strain pulp through a medium-holed sieve. (Traditionally a piece of netting, such as was used to make mosquito netting, served the purpose.)
4. Spread a piece of white muslin or thin white cotton cloth on a tray. Spread pulp thinly on cloth and sun-dry it.
5. Repeat steps 2 and 3 on the following day.
6. Spread another layer of palmyra fruit pulp equally thinly over the previous one. Leave to dry in the sun.
7. Repeat the process for 6 or 7 days till the pinaatu is about an inch thick.
8. Dry for another couple of days or until it is not sticky to the touch.
9. Remove the cloth by sprinkling water over it and peeling the pinaatu away.
10. Dry out the pinaatu further.
11. Cut into pieces and store till needed.

Paani Pinaatu

3 cups pinaatu pieces
2 dessertspoons oil
1½ cups tiny slivers of coconut
¾ cup sesame seeds (less rather than more)
3 cups crushed palm sugar pieces (panangkatti)
¾ cup water
¾ tsp ground pepper
¾ tsp ground cumin

METHOD

1. Heat oil in a pan. Fry coconut pieces till golden. Drain on absorbent paper.
2. In the same oil, fry sesame seeds till golden and drain at once.
3. To make the syrup, dissolve palm sugar pieces in water over a low flame. The syrup should be thick enough to be sticky (similar to golden syrup or honey). Remove from flame and set aside to cool.
4. In a bowl, mix well together, pieces of pinaatu, coconut and sesame seeds, ground pepper, ground cumin and palm sugar syrup.
5. Traditionally, pani pinaatu was stored in an earthenware pot. A muslin cloth was tied over the mouth, to let it 'breathe', reducing the chances of deterioration.

Odiyal Dosa

Odiyalmaa Thosai

1 cup palmyra root (odiyal) flour
1 cup split black gram (urad dal)
2 cups rice flour
1 tsp baking powder

METHOD

1. Soak split black gram for a couple of hours.
2. Grind fine.
3. Soak odiyal flour. Drain the water. Repeat a couple of times.
4. Strain through a muslin cloth to remove all water.
5. Mix odiyal flour with ground black gram well.
6. Add rice flour and baking powder.
7. Mix well and set aside to ferment for at least 7 hours.
8. Heat a skillet and brush it with oil. Add a little water to the dough, if necessary.
9. Spoon a ladleful on to the skillet and spread to form a circle. Cook as you would, a normal rice flour thosai.

Panangkilangu Thuvayal

6 boiled panangkilangu (root of the palmyra seedling)
6–8 dried chillies
¼ tsp salt
1 tsp pepper
½ grated coconut

METHOD

1. Split the panangkilangu in half. Remove the centre vein and break into pieces. Tear as much fibre away from it as possible.
2. Pound or grind together, dried chillies, salt and pepper.
3. Add the panangkilangu pieces.
4. Add the grated coconut.
5. Pound or grind well. Remove and form into little balls and serve as a snack.

Pulukkodiyal Laddu

1 cup pulukkodiyal or 1 cup pulukkodiyal flour
½ cup palm jaggery
½ cup grated coconut
a pinch salt

METHOD

1. Split each pulukkodiyal into two. Remove the vein. Break into pieces, tearing off fibres as you go along. Grind into flour.
2. Pound or grind together, pulukkodiyal flour, jaggery, grated coconut and salt.
3. Form into balls. Serve as a snack.

Savoury Pulukkodiyal Balls

Pulukkodiyal Thuvayal

1 cup pulukkodiyal flour
1 cup grated coconut
3 or 4 green chillies, chopped
1 medium-sized onion, chopped
1 dessertspoon ground pepper
A pinch salt

METHOD

1. Pound or grind all ingredients together.
2. Form into balls. Serve as a snack.

Pulukkodiyal-Semolina Laddu

Pulukkodiyal Ravai Laddu

1 cup pulukkodiyal flour
20 sultanas
15–18 cashew nuts, chopped
1 cup semolina, lightly roasted
1 cup grated coconut
2 cups sugar
1 tsp ghee or butter

1 cup milk
1 dessertspoon vanilla essence

METHOD

1. Heat ghee in a pan. Lightly fry sultanas and cashew nuts.
2. Add semolina. Fry a little. Remove into a bowl.
3. Roast grated coconut in a pan. Add to semolina mixture.
4. Add sugar and pulukkodiyal flour to semolina mixture. Mix all together.
5. Heat a pan and add a teaspoon of ghee or butter.
6. Return the mixture to the pan. Add milk and vanilla essence. Mix well and remove from flame.
7. Form into balls and serve as a snack.

Pulukkodiyal Vadai

1 cup split black gram flour
1 cup plain flour
1 cup pulukkodiyal flour
¼ tsp salt
1 dessertspoon fennel seeds
8 dried red chillies
Oil for frying

METHOD

1. Soak black gram for about two hours. Grind coarsely.
2. Add plain flour, pulukkodiyal flour, salt and fennel seeds.
3. Grind or pound dried chillies and add to mixture.
4. Form small round shapes with your hands and deep-fry.
5. Serve hot as a snack.

Palmyra Pulp Thosai

Panangkali Thosai

1 cup palmyra fruit pulp
4 cups plain flour or rice flour
1 tsp cumin seeds
¼ tsp salt
1 tsp pepper
Gingelly oil to grease skillet

METHOD

1. Mix palmyra fruit pulp and plain flour. Set aside to ferment for at least 8 hours in a warm place.
2. Add cumin seeds, salt and pepper. Add a little water if mixture is too thick.
3. Heat a skillet and grease it with gingelly oil.
4. Spoon a ladleful of fermented pulp onto centre of skillet and spread it with ladle to form a circle. Turn over and cook.
5. Remove and serve with coconut chutney.

Palmyra Fruit Payasam

Panampala Payasam

Pulp of 3 palmyra fruits
½ cup black gram flour (urad dal)
2 cups milk
3 dessertspoons sugar
20 cashew nuts, chopped
20 sultanas
2½ tsp vanilla essence

METHOD

1. Mix well together palmyra fruit pulp and black gram flour.
2. Place milk and sugar in a pan and bring to boil.
3. Add palmyra fruit mixture and cook together, stirring constantly to avoid forming lumps.
4. Add cashew nuts, sultanas and vanilla essence. Cook till it thickens a little.
5. Remove and serve warm as a dessert.

Vattalappam

500 gm palmyra palm jaggery
3 cups thick coconut milk
8 eggs
¼ tsp grated nutmeg
¼ tsp ground cinnamon
13–15 cashew nuts, split

METHOD

1. Mix palmyra palm jaggery and coconut milk.
2. Beat yolks and whites of eggs separately. Mix both together and beat well.
3. Add beaten eggs to coconut milk mixture. Stir well to dissolve jaggery and mix eggs.
4. Add nutmeg and cinnamon.
5. Pour into dish. Decorate the top with cashew nuts.
6. Steam till firm. Serve cool.

This pudding, traditionally a Sinhalese dish, has become an integral part of Tamil cuisine.

Pulukkodiyal Alwa

Pulukkodiyalmaa Aluva

1 cup pulukkodiyal flour
1½ cups sugar
1 tsp cardamom powder
1 tsp vanilla essence
1 dessertspoon ghee or butter

METHOD

1. Heat sugar till it is of thin wire consistency. (See glossary of cooking terms.)
2. Add pulukkodiyal flour, a little at a time, stirring the while.
3. Add cardamom powder and vanilla essence. Add ghee and keep turning over until mixture leaves the sides of the pan.
4. Put into a greased dish. Cut and serve when cool.

Pulukkodiyal Flour Cookies

Odiyal Kokis

425 gm plain flour
75 gm pulukkodiyal flour
250 gm butter or margarine
320 gm castor sugar
1 tsp baking powder
1 tsp vanilla essence

METHOD

1. Cream butter or margarine and castor sugar together.
2. Sift plain and pulukkodiyal flour and baking powder together.

3. Add to creamed butter and sugar.
4. Add vanilla essence.
5. Fold in with a metal spoon to mix well.
6. Roll out dough and cut into desired shapes for cookies.
7. Bake in a moderate oven till golden.

Palmyra Fruit Dodol

Panangkali Dodol

1 cup palmyra fruit pulp
1 cup thin coconut milk
50 gm brown sugar
½ cup rice flour
100 gm palm jaggery pieces
50 gm sago
1 cup thick coconut milk
50 gm cashew nuts

METHOD

1. Mix palmyra fruit pulp in thin coconut milk. Add brown sugar, rice flour and palm jaggery.
2. Mix well and place pan on flame. Cook, stirring all the time, until oil oozes out. Remove excess oil with a spoon.
3. Add sago and continue to cook. Add thick coconut milk and stir continuously.
4. Add chopped cashew nuts. Continue to remove excess oil with a spoon.
5. When mixture is cooked enough to leave the sides of the pan, remove from the flame.
6. Dish on to a tray and cut into squares when cool.

Palmyra Fruit Cake

Panangkali Cake

1 cup palmyra fruit pulp
250 gm butter
250 gm castor sugar
5 eggs
250 gm plain flour

1 tsp baking powder
2 tsp vanilla essence

METHOD

1. Cream butter and castor sugar together.
2. Add eggs, one at a time. Beat thoroughly and set aside.
3. Sift flour and baking powder together.
4. Add to the creamed mixture and fold in with a metal spoon. Mix well.
5. Add palmyra fruit pulp.
6. Add vanilla essence.
7. Mix well and pour into a greased and lined baking dish.
8. Bake in a moderate oven for approximately 30 minutes.

Pulukkodiyal Flour Butter Cake

Pulukkodiyal Maa Butter Cake

250 gm soft brown sugar
250 gm butter
4 eggs
1 tsp baking powder
200 gm plain flour
50 gm pulukkodiyal flour
1 tsp vanilla essence

METHOD

1. Cream together sugar and butter till fluffy.
2. Add eggs, one at a time, beating each thoroughly into mixture.
3. Sift together baking powder, plain and odiyal flour twice.
4. Add to creamed mixture, a little at a time, folding in with a metal spoon.
5. Add vanilla essence, mixing well.
6. Pour into a greased, lined baking dish.
7. Bake in a moderate oven for approximately 30 minutes.

Palakarams and other Teatime Treats

Black Gram Vadai
Spinach Vadai
Bengal Gram Vadai
Potato Bonda

Pal Roti
Kolukattai
Mothagam
String Hopper Kolukattai
Pidi Kolukattai

Ariyatharam
Murukku
Chippi
Sitrundi

Paitham-urundai
Pahoda
Omapodi
Kaaraampuundhi
"Mixture"

Semolina Laddu
Rice Flakes Laddu
Black Gram and Rice Flour Porridge
Sesame Seed Sweet
Sweet Sesame Balls

Porivilaanggaai
Uudumaa Kool
Fried Sesame Seed Flour Snack
Black Gram and Rice Fried Flour Snack
Green Gram and Rice Flour Snack

Egg Uluthamaa Varuval
Bengal Gram Susiyam
Potato Alwa
Tapioca Thuvayal
Dodol
Coconut Rock

Black Gram Vadai

Ulunthu Vadai

1 cup dehusked black gram (urad dal)
1 onion, chopped fine
2 green chillies, chopped fine
4–5 curry leaves, chopped fine
½ tsp salt
Oil for frying

METHOD

1. Soak black gram overnight or for at least 4 hours.
2. Drain and grind to a coarse paste.
3. Add chopped onion, chillies, curry leaves and salt. Mix well.
4. To make each vadai, roughly roll a small piece of dough into a ball. Place it in the palm of your hand and flatten it. Make a hole (doughnut-like) in the centre with your index finger.
5. Deep-fry the vadai in oil until golden, turning to cook evenly on both sides (about 5 minutes).

Spinach Vadai

Keera Vadai

2 cups finely chopped tender spinach leaves
½ cup split, black gram (urad dal)
1 dessertspoon green chillies, chopped
1 large onion, chopped fine

1 tsp chopped ginger
6–8 curry leaves, chopped fine
1 dessertspoon grated coconut
½ tsp salt
Oil for frying

METHOD

1. Soak black gram for 2–3 hours. Grind fairly fine.
2. Heat oil. Fry green chillies, chopped onion, ginger and curry leaves.
3. Add spinach. Cook till it softens.
4. Add to black gram mixture.
5. Add grated coconut and salt. Mix well.
6. Form into little patties on the palm of your hand or on a greased banana leaf. Make a hole (doughnut-like) in the centre.
7. Deep-fry and drain from oil when golden.
8. Serve on its own or with a preferred chutney.

Bengal Gram Vadai

Kadalai Vadai

1 cup Bengal gram
3–5 chillies, chopped fine
2 dessertspoons chilli powder
1 medium-sized onion, chopped fine
5–8 curry leaves, chopped fine
½ tsp salt
Oil for frying

METHOD

1. Soak Bengal gram for two hours. Grind coarsely.
2. Add all the ingredients and mix well.
3. Heat oil in a wok.
4. Form the mixture into little patties and deep-fry. Drain when golden and well cooked.

Potato Bonda

Urulakkilangu Bonda

500 gm potatoes, boiled, peeled and mashed
A pinch of turmeric
½ tsp chilli powder
½ tsp fennel seed powder
A tiny piece of asafoetida, soaked in a tsp warm water,
    or ¼ tsp asafoetida powder
½ tsp salt
1 tsp oil ⎫
1 tsp mustard seeds |
8–10 green chillies, chopped |
¼ cup onions, chopped ⎬ for seasoning
½ tsp chopped ginger |
1 sprig curry leaves, chopped fine ⎭
¼ cup long grain rice flour ⎫
¾ cup Bengal gram flour |
¼ tsp baking powder ⎬ for batter
A pinch of salt |
Oil for frying ⎭

METHOD

1. To the mashed potatoes, add turmeric, chilli powder, fennel seed powder, asafoetida and salt.
2. Heat a little oil in a pan. Add mustard seeds, green chillies, onions, ginger and curry leaves.
3. Add to the mashed potatos and mix well.
4. Form into lime-sized balls.
5. To make the batter mix all the ingredients. Add enough water to make a smooth batter.
6. Heat oil in a wok.
7. Dip potato balls in batter and deep-fry.
8. When golden brown, drain on absorbent paper.
9. Serve warm.

Pal Roti

1 cup uncooked rice, soaked in water for at least an hour
1 cup coconut milk
1 tbsp white sesame seeds

½ tsp salt
½ cup water
Oil for frying

METHOD

1. Grind ½ cup rice coarsely, slightly grainy in texture. Separately grind the remaining rice very fine. Mix the two.
2. Boil rice, coconut milk, sesame seeds, salt and water together. Stir while boiling.
3. Remove and let it stand for about 15–20 minutes.
4. Make small balls (about 3 cm diameter). Roll out each on a piece of oiled banana leaf or on greaseproof paper. Alternatively, put each in the centre of your palm and press out into a circular shape with the other palm.
5. Heat oil and fry balls till golden. Work oil over each roti. Turn each over to cook evenly.
6. Remove from oil and drain on absorbent paper.

Kolukattai

These steamed dumplings are shaped like half-moons with the curved edge fashioned beautifully into 'teeth'. In a charming ceremony to celebrate the emergence of teeth in an infant, the baby is seated on a white cloth and another piece of cloth is draped on his/her head. A few Kolukattais are dropped on the infant's head to wish the child perfect teeth—as perfect as the sweet dumplings!

1 cup roasted rice flour
½ cup split green gram (moong dal), roasted
1½ cups scraped (grated) coconut
1 cup jaggery pieces, crushed
8 cardamom seeds, pounded fine
1 tsp salt
1½ cups water
A little ghee or coconut oil

METHOD

1. Boil green gram in water till cooked but firm.
2. Drain, spread gram on a tray and allow to cool.
3. When cool, add coconut, jaggery and cardamom powder and mix with a spoon.
4. Add salt to the rice flour and mix with boiling water till it is smooth but firm enough to form a ball.
5. Grease your hand using very little ghee or coconut oil to shape the dough into lime-sized balls.
6. Press the ball out into a bowl-like shape using your fingers.
7. Place 1½ –2 teaspoons of gram mixture in the 'bowl'.

8. Close to form a semi-circular shape. Seal edges by turning one edge over in a 'teeth-like' pattern.
9. Alternatively, a kolukattai ural will make this easy work!

Mothagam

Mothagams are round dumplings with the edges pulled together to form a cone. These are believed to be dearly loved by Ganesha, the elephant-headed deity, who holds a mothagam in one of his hands. Mothagams are offered to him in worship.

Follow Steps 1–7 for kolukattai.

8. Close by bringing the edges together to form a small cone at the top.
9. Steam as for kolukattai.

String Hopper Kolukattai

Idi-appa Kolukattai

Ingredients as for kolukattai.

METHOD
1. Mix flour as for kolukattai.
2. Using a string hopper ural, make string hoppers about 4–5 centimetres in diameter on a piece of greased banana leaf or greased baking paper. (For recipe for String Hoppers see p. 2.)
3. Mix the filling as for kolukattai.
4. Place 2 teaspoons of filling on one half of the centre of the string hopper.
5. Fold each string hopper over to form a semi-circle.
6. Lift carefully on to a steaming tray and steam as for string hoppers (p. 2).
7. Remove when not sticky to touch.

Note: If green gram is not desired, string hoppers can be filled with a syrup.

SYRUP FILLING

½ cup jaggery
1¾ dessertspoons water
1 cup grated coconut
1 small piece cinnamon
½ tsp rice flour
Salt to taste

METHOD

1. Make syrup by boiling jaggery and water.
2. Remove from stove and add all other ingredients. Mix well.

Pidi Kolukattai

½ cup split green gram (moong dal), roasted
2 cups rice flour, slightly roasted
2 cups scraped (grated) coconut
½ cup jaggery cut into pieces
½ tsp salt
1½ cups water
Jaggery syrup (jaggery and ½ cup water boiled and cooled)

METHOD

1. Boil green gram in water till cooked firm (not mushy)
2. Drain. When cool, add flour, coconut, jaggery pieces and salt. Mix well.
3. Make elongated, oval shapes with fingers. Make indentations with three fingers.
4. Place on a steaming tray. Add syrup into the indentations and steam till cooked.

Ariyatharam

A typical Jaffna sweet which is eaten as a teatime fried 'cake'.

2 cups rice
1 tsp salt
1 tsp sesame seeds
2 tbsp ghee
½ cup water
2 cups sugar
Oil for frying

METHOD

1. Soak rice overnight.
2. Drain water and pound or grind rice in a food processor.
3. Sieve ground rice.
4. Add salt, sesame seeds and ghee. Mix well together.
5. Add ½ cup water to the sugar and boil.
   (To check for consistency, drop a little sugar syrup into a cup of water. If it forms into a ball, turn off flame.)

6. Pour into rice mixture and mix it into a dough.
7. Cover and set aside for 3 hours.
8. Once dough has hardened, roll into small balls. Flatten each in the palm of your hand with a little oil.
9. Deep-fry in hot oil.
10. Can be served warm but tastes just as good even a day later.

Murukku*

2 cups roasted rice flour
½ cup roasted black gram (urad dal) flour
1½ tbsp sesame seeds
1½ tsp salt
½ tsp pepper
1 tsp cumin seeds
1½ cups coconut milk
Oil for frying

*A murukku ural (pressing mould) is essential and may be purchased in stores selling Indian and Sri Lankan groceries.

METHOD

1. Mix together rice flour, black gram flour, sesame seeds, salt, pepper and cumin seeds.
2. Boil coconut milk.
3. Pour it into the mixture and make into a dough.
4. Press dough through murukku mould on to squares of greaseproof paper.
5. Lift off the paper and lower into hot oil. Fry till golden.
6. Drain and store in an airtight container.

Chippi (Achu Palakaram)

2 cups rice flour, roasted
4 cups thin coconut milk (3 cups thick coconut milk to 1 cup water)
1 tsp salt
3 dessertspoons black gram (urad dal) flour, roasted
2 dessertspoons white sesame seeds
½ tsp powdered cardamom seeds

Oil for frying
1½ cups sugar
½ cup water

*A 'Chippi' mould is required. If not available, a fork will do.

METHOD

1. Boil the coconut milk and salt.
2. Put the rice flour into a bowl. Make a well in the centre and pour the boiling coconut milk into it. Mix thoroughly. Allow to cool for a couple of minutes.
3. Add gram flour, sesame seeds and cardamom powder. Mix well.
4. Form tiny balls. Press each against a greased chippi mould or fork, and roll it over to form a shell shape (hence the name, chippi or 'shell').
5. Deep-fry till all are done. Remove from oil and set aside in a large bowl.
6. To make the syrup, bring sugar and water to boil. To check the consistency put a drop in cold water. If the syrup does not dissolve then it is the correct consistency. Stir the syrup well.
7. Pour over chippis and mix quickly to coat evenly before sugar crystallises.

Sitrundi

These are small half-moon shaped biscuit patties, filled with a sweet mixture. A sitrundi ural set makes easy work of these very attractive, filled biscuits.

1 cup green gram (moong dal) flour
1 dessertspoon ghee
2 dessertspoons cashew nuts crushed (optional)
2 cups castor sugar
½ tsp cardamom powder
2 cups long grained rice, soaked for two hours
½ cup light coconut milk
½ tsp salt
4 dessertspoons black gram (urad dal) flour, roasted
1 cup water
Oil for frying
A sitrundi ural set (if available)

METHOD

1. To prepare the filling, heat ghee in a pan. Add cashew nuts (if being used) and roast till golden brown. Mix together with gram flour, sugar and cardamom powder.

2. To prepare the dough, drain the rice and grind finely. Put it through a medium-holed sieve. Set aside the grainy parts. Grind the rest very fine.
3. Remove and roast slightly. Add the grainy flour to this.
4. In a heavy pan, boil coconut milk and salt. Remove.
5. Add to the roasted rice flour a little at a time, stirring to make sure that it is mixed properly and does not form lumps. Set aside to cool for about 20 minutes.
6. Add black gram flour and knead well, dipping fingers in ghee to facilitate the mixing.
7. If a sitrundi mould is available, fill each with ½ teaspoon of filling.
8. If a mould is not available, roll out dough and cut tiny circles about 2 inches in diameter. Hold each in your palm and fill using the filling. Seal, making fluted decorative designs.
9. Heat oil. Deep-fry till golden.
10. Remove from oil and drain on absorbent paper.
11. Keeps for several weeks in an airtight container.

Paitham-urundai (Paitham-paniyaram)

Traditionally, an ural, a wooden pounding instrument, is used to pound the ingredients. Today a grinder or even a food processor may serve the purpose. Hence the use below, of the word 'grind' rather than 'pound'.

¼ cup long grained rice
¾ cup grated coconut
1 cup green gram flour
½ tsp cumin seeds
¼ tsp pepper
1¼ cup sugar
½ cup water
½ cup long grained rice flour ⎫
½ cup light coconut milk   ⎬ for batter
¾ tsp salt   ⎭
Oil for frying

METHOD

1. Soak rice for a couple of hours. Grind fine.
2. Roast grated coconut in a dry pan till very light golden.
3. Grind a little.
4. Add ground rice, gram flour, roasted coconut, cumin seeds and pepper. Grind together well. Remove and put into a bowl that is wide enough to work in with your hands.

5. Make a syrup by dissolving sugar in water over a low flame.
6. Add to ground mixture and mix well quickly.
7. Form into small, firm balls.
8. Mix ingredients for batter well, making sure there are no lumps.
9. Heat oil. Dip balls in batter and fry till golden.
10. Drain on absorbent paper.

These are normally made a week ahead for a special occasion and are eaten cold.

Pahoda

1 cup Bengal gram flour (besan)
½ cup long grained rice flour
2 tsp chopped green chillies
2 dessertspoons chopped onions
1 tsp chopped ginger
2 tsp chilli powder
½ tsp fennel seed powder
1 sprig curry leaves, chopped fine
1 tsp salt
Oil for frying

METHOD
1. Soak Bengal gram for two to three hours. Grind coarsely.
2. Add all other ingredients and continue to grind till gram is smooth.
3. Heat oil in a wok.
4. Drop dessertspoonsfuls of the mixture into the hot oil.
5. Fry till golden brown. Drain on absorbent paper.

Omapodi

An 'ural' like the one used to make murukkus is required to make omapodi. Sometimes a base ural can be bought with different moulds, including the one for omapodi.

1 cup Bengal gram flour (besan)
½ cup rice flour
1½ tsp omam (ajwain) powder
1 tsp chilli powder
2 tsp coconut oil

A tiny piece of asafoetida
A pinch of baking powder
1 tsp salt

METHOD

1. Mix all the ingredients together.
2. Heat oil in a kadai (wok).
3. Using an omapodi ural, squeeze out the mixture straight into the oil.
4. Drain as soon as it turns golden. (It cooks fast so be careful not to let it turn a dark brown.)
5. Drain on absorbent paper.

Kaaraampuundhi

You will need a large flat ladle with holes (such as used for draining) or a small steaming tray with fine holes to pour the kaaraampuundhi mixture into the oil.

½ cup Bengal gram flour (besan)
¼ cup unroasted rice flour
½ tsp chilli powder
¾ cup water
Salt to taste
Oil for frying

METHOD

1. Mix all ingredients together well.
2. Heat oil in a wok.
3. Take a ladleful of the mixture and pass it through the perforated spoon or tray so that small droplets fall into the oil.
4. Drain as soon as they turn golden. These cook very fast so be prepared to drain them immediately on to absorbent paper.

"Mixture"

This dish being exactly what its name suggests, is a combination of many titbits. These vary according to individual taste. But the basic components are omapodi and kaaraampuundhi. To these may be added a variety of things. Some suggestions are given below.

3 teacups omapodi
3 teacups kaaraampuundhi
2 potatoes

1 cup rice flakes (aval)
1 cup cashew nuts, halved
1 sprig curry leaves, cut fine
3 dried red chillies
A small piece of asafoetida
A handful of roasted peanuts, skinned and halved
A handful of sultanas
1 tsp salt

METHOD

Ingredients to be deep-fried:

Potatoes: Peel and cut into 1 inch julienne strips. Deep-fry. Drain and set aside.

Rice flakes: Deep-fry very quickly. Drain and set aside.

Cashew nuts: Deep-fry. Drain and set aside.

Curry leaves: Deep-fry quickly, drain and set aside.

1. Roast and pound dried chillies and asafoetida.
2. Mix in a bowl omapodi, kaaraampuundhi, fried ingredients, peanuts, sultanas and ground ingredients. Add salt.
3. Add all the fried ingredients. Mix well together.
4. Store in an airtight container and serve when required.

Note: Unless stored in an airtight container, the "mixture" will turn soft.

Semolina Laddu

Rava Laddu

1 cup semolina
2 tbsp ghee
10 cashew nuts cut into little pieces
1 dessertspoon sultanas, cut into small pieces
1 cup grated coconut
1 cup castor sugar
1 cup or a little more milk
1 tsp powdered cardamom seeds
¼ tsp powdered cloves

METHOD

1. Heat ghee in a pan and fry cashew nuts and sultanas. Remove and set aside.
2. Put the semolina into the same pan and fry it until it gets warm. Add the grated coconut and fry over a low flame till light golden.

3. Add sugar, fried cashews and sultanas, milk, cardamom and clove powder.
4. Fry until the sugar begins to dissolve. Turn off flame.
5. Take spoonfuls of the hot mixture and roll between floured hands to form balls, when the heat is bearable.
6. Store in an airtight container and serve when required.

Should the mixture become too dry sprinkle some warm water and mix to soften. The balls have to be made quickly before the mixture cools.

Rice Flakes Laddu

Aval Laddu

1 cup rice flakes (aval)
1 cup castor sugar
¼ tsp cardamom powder
2 dessertspoons cashew nuts, roasted, chopped
¾ cup ghee

METHOD
1. Roast and grind rice flakes.
2. Pound or grind together sugar and cardamom powder.
3. Add chopped cashew nuts.
4. Heat the ghee.
5. Mix all the ingredients with the ground rice flakes.
6. Form into lime-sized balls.
7. Store in an airtight container and serve when required.

Black Gram and Rice Flour Porridge

Uluthammaa Kadzhi

The word 'porridge' is used loosely here. 'Kadzhi' is really a cooked paste.

2 cups unroasted rice flour
¾ cup roasted black gram (urad dal) flour
½ tsp salt
½ cup thin coconut milk
2 tbsp jaggery or sugar (optional)
½ cup thick coconut milk

METHOD

1. Dissolve both flours and salt in a pan of thin coconut milk.
2. Place the pan on the stove and bring ingredients to boil, stirring constantly to avoid forming lumps.
3. If you want it sweet, add sugar or jaggery once the mixture begins to thicken.
4. Add thick coconut milk. When porridge thickens, remove from stove.
5. Spread mixture on a plate to cool.

Sesame Seed Sweet

Ellu Pahu

1 cup white sesame seeds
1½ cups jaggery pieces
1 tsp ghee
¼ cup water

METHOD

1. Heat ghee in a pan. Fry sesame seeds till golden.
2. Spread sesame seeds on a greased plate.
3. Boil jaggery pieces in water. To check consistency, put a drop of jaggery syrup in cold water. It should not dissolve.
4. Pour jaggery syrup over sesame seeds, making sure all are covered. Smooth over the top.
5. When cooled, cut into bite-sized pieces.

VARIATIONS

Sesame Seed Balls: These can also be made into tiny balls: Place fried sesame seeds in a bowl. Pour dissolved jaggery over sesame seeds. Mix and form into very small balls, about 2 cm in diameter.

Groundnut Sweet: Shelled, roasted groundnuts can be used in the same way.

Sweet Sesame Balls

Ellu Urundai

The best results are obtained if sesame seeds are pounded in the traditional way. It is then that the 'good oil' (gingelly oil) oozes from the sesame seed.

Gingelly oil is much prized in Tamil cuisine. In fact, elders say "The money given to the doctor would have been better spent at the (gingelly) oilmonger." In many villages the oilmonger has an almost primitive way of grinding sesame seeds with the use of an ox, moving round and round, extracting the 'Nalla-ennai' literally the 'good oil'. Much faith (and not without reason) is placed on the health-enhancing properties of this oil. These sesame balls, therefore, are eaten (one a day) in the interests of enduring health.

> 1 cup white sesame seeds
> ½ cup black gram flour, roasted
> 1 cup castor sugar
> A little hot water

METHOD

1. Pound sesame seeds, dribbling a little (very little) water just to keep wetting it.
2. Add the black gram flour and continue pounding.
3. Add sugar. Pound till it is well mixed.
4. Remove and form into balls. If well pounded the balls will ooze sesame (gingelly) oil.
5. Store in an airtight jar and use as required.

Porivilaanggaai

> 1¼ cups split green gram (moong dal), roasted
> ½ cup Bengal gram (channa dal)
> ½ cup semolina
> ¼ cup white sesame seeds
> a pinch cardamom powder
> 2½ cups jaggery pieces
> 2½ dessertspoons water
> ¼ cup tiny slices of coconut

METHOD

1. Roast Bengal gram and semolina. Remove and add roasted green gram.
2. Grind all three together.
3. Roast sesame seeds and cardamom powder.
4. Add to the ground mixture.
5. Make syrup by boiling water and jaggery together. To check the consistency put a drop in water. The drop should not dissolve.
6. Add to the mixture of gram, semolina and sesame seeds. Add the slices of coconut.
7. Mix well and form into lime-sized balls.

Uudumaa Kool

1 cup parboiled rice
150 gm jaggery
2 tsp roasted split green gram (moong dal)
1½ dessertspoons tiny slices of coconut
4 cups water
½ cup coconut milk
1 tsp salt
¼ tsp pepper
¼ tsp cumin seed powder

METHOD

1. Soak the parboiled rice for 1–2 hours. Drain and grind without adding any water.
2. With ¼ of the ground rice make small balls and set aside.
3. In 2 cups water boil the rice balls, roasted green gram and slices of coconut.
4. Mix the remaining rice mixture and jaggery in 2 cup of water. Bring to boil in another pan.
5. Pour into rice ball mixture and add coconut milk. Stir to make sure it does not form lumps.
6. Once boiled add salt, pepper, cumin seed powder and jaggery. Turn off the flame and remove.

This is like a sweet rice porridge.

Fried Sesame Seeds Flour Snack

Ellu Pori-arisi Maa

These snacks are among the health foods of Tamil cuisine. Young people are fed on these for stamina and health. Youthful memories testify to its keeping qualities.

2 cups parboiled rice
2 cups sesame seeds
2 cups jaggery pieces

METHOD

1. Roast rice and grind it.
2. Roast sesame seeds and grind.
3. Mix together the ground rice, ground sesame seeds and jaggery pieces.
4. Grind all together.
5. Store and serve as a health snack.

Black Gram and Rice Fried Flour Snack

Uluthammaa Seintha Varuval Maa

Recalling memories of a past age, Dr Kanthi Kanavathipillai said, "When we went to study in India, our mothers used to pack a huge cloth bag of this snack for each of us. It would last us for three months. As we travelled by ship across the Straits each young university student could almost be identified by the uluthammaa varuval bag that was part of his or her student paraphernalia."

1 cup roasted rice flour
¾ cup milk (cow's milk or coconut milk)
¼ cup gingelly oil
¼ cup ghee
½ cup black gram flour (uluthammaa), well-roasted
¾ cup castor sugar

METHOD

1. Mix milk and flour to a paste, dry enough to form a grainy texture (like puttu).
2. Heat gingelly oil and ghee in a wok, over a low flame.
3. Add milk and flour mixture. Fry gently, turning constantly, being careful not to let it burn.
4. When mixture turns golden, add black gram flour.
5. Add sugar. Mix well and remove from flame.
6. When cool, serve as a health snack.

Green Gram and Rice Flour Snack

Paithamaa Sentha Pori-arisi Maa

2 cups parboiled rice
1 cup roasted green gram flour
½ cup white sesame seeds
1 cup grated coconut
1½ cups castor sugar
¼ cup ghee

METHOD

1. Roast rice till golden. Remove and grind fine into flour.
2. Roast sesame seeds till light golden. Pound or grind fine.
3. Roast grated coconut till light golden. Pound or grind fine.
4. Mix ground rice flour, green gram flour, ground sesame seeds, ground coconut and castor sugar.

5. Heat ghee in a pan.
6. Add all the ingredients to the ghee. Mix well. Pound together again if necessary.
7. Store in an airtight container. Will keep for at least three months.

Egg Uluthamaa Varuval

Muttai Maa

"Egg Uluthammaa Varuval" is an important part of the diet of girls who have just attained puberty. They are also required to consume a raw egg and gingelly oil.

"I'll never forget that awful early morning ritual. One raw egg, and the egg shell filled with gingelly oil to follow!! But I am grateful for it now that I am in my forties. It must have something to do with the sustained energy I feel even after four children." A common sentiment frequently expressed in general conversations among the women of Jaffna.

1 cup roasted rice flour
¾ cup milk (cow's milk or coconut milk)
2 large or 3 small eggs
¼ cup gingelly oil
¼ cup ghee
½ cup black gram flour (uluthammaa), well-roasted
¾ cup castor sugar
1 tsp vanilla essence or ¼ tsp ground cardamom seeds

METHOD

1. Mix milk and flour to a paste, dry enough to form a grainy texture (like puttu).
2. Beat eggs lightly. Add to milk and flour mixture.
3. Heat gingelly oil and ghee in a wok, over a low flame.
4. Add the milk, egg and flour mixture. Fry gently, turning constantly, being careful not to let it burn.
5. When it turns golden, add black gram flour and sugar.
6. Add vanilla essence or cardamom powder. Mix well and remove from flame.
7. When cool, serve as health snack.

Bengal Gram Susiyam

Kadala-maa Susiyam

1½ cups Bengal gram (channa dal)
1½ cups grated coconut

1½ cups jaggery pieces
¼ tsp cardamom powder
3 cups plain flour
3 cups coconut milk ⎫
¼ tsp baking powder ⎬ for batter
½ tsp salt ⎭

METHOD

1. Boil Bengal gram. When soft, drain water.
2. Lower flame and add grated coconut, jaggery and cardamom powder.
3. Mix well.
4. When it begins to dry out, remove from flame.
5. Grind and roll into lime-sized balls.
6. To make batter, mix all the ingredients together. Add more flour if thicker batter is required.
7. Dip balls in batter and deep-fry till golden.
8. Drain on absorbent paper and serve.

Potato Alwa

Urulakkilangu Aluva

250 gm potatoes (approximately)
500 gm sugar
½ cup water
2 dessertspoons butter or ghee
¼ cup cashew nuts, chopped
¼ cup sultanas, halved
½ tsp vanilla essence

METHOD

1. Boil, peel and mash potatoes.
2. Boil sugar in water, till syrup is of thread-like consistency. (When a drop of it is taken between thumb and index finger and pulled apart, it forms a thread.)
3. Remove from stove.
4. Add potatoes and butter.
5. When it begins to firm, add cashew nuts, sultanas and vanilla essence.
6. Stir till mixture leaves the sides of the pan.
7. Spread on a shallow tray. Cut into pieces and serve.

Tapioca Thuvayal

Maravalli Thuvayal

500 gm tapioca
10 medium-sized green chillies
1 small onion, quartered
1 tsp salt
1 cup grated coconut
1 sprig curry leaves

METHOD

1. Peel and cut tapioca. Boil till soft.
2. Pound or grind together green chillies, onions and salt.
3. Add tapioca and continue to pound or grind.
4. Add grated coconut and pound well together. Add curry leaves.
5. Remove and form into balls. Serve as a snack.
6. Will not keep for more than a day or two.

Dodol

Thothol

Tamil cuisine has borrowed from the food traditions of other people of Sri Lanka, including the Muslim Malay community. Dodol is one such dish that has become a part of Tamil cuisine.

5½ cups thick coconut milk
¾ cup long grained rice flour
½ cup plain flour
½ tsp salt
750 gm jaggery or sugar
½ tsp cardamom seed powder
25 cashew nuts, roasted and chopped

METHOD

1. In 2 cups of coconut milk, mix rice flour, plain flour, salt and jaggery.
2. Bring the remaining coconut milk to boil.
3. Add flour mixture, stirring continuously.
4. Stir continuously till mixture leaves the sides of the pan. Remove excess oil as it emerges from coconut milk.

5. Add cardamom powder and cashew nuts.
6. Remove any excess oil from dodol as it surfaces.
7. Turn off the flame.
8. Dish out the dodol into a colander or sieve to drain any excess oil that may remain.
9. When cool cut into squares and serve.
10. Can be stored for a week or so.

Coconut Rock

Thenggapuu Aluva

1½ cups grated coconut
½ tin condensed milk
1 cup sugar
¼ cup water
2 tsp vanilla
Colouring if desired. Usually red or green is preferred.

METHOD

1. Put all ingredients in a pan. Stir continuously on a low flame to make sure the mixture does not burn. Add colouring if desired.
2. After it reaches 'soft-ball stage' (a small lump put in cold water holds its shape), cook for a further three minutes.
3. Remove and dish into a greased tray. Allow to set and cut into squares.
4. Keeps well for several weeks.

Sweets and Desserts

Tapioca Kool
Aadi Kool
Kesari
Sago Payasam

Rice Payasam
Vermicelli Payasam
Green Gram Payasam
Fried String Hoppers in Syrup

Jaggery Pudding
Purple Yam Pudding
Rock Sugar Kool
Wood-Apple Cream

The sweets tradition of Tamils (and of several Indian communities) varies somewhat from the Western tradition where they are eaten at the end of a meal. Here a small sweet, usually a slice of something sweet is served at the beginning of a meal. But with cross-cultural influences, sweets seem to be arriving at Tamil tables in the conventional Western way—as dessert.

In their sweets the Tamils in the North and East of Sri Lanka have been influenced greatly by the Sinhalese, Malays and Europeans. While many are part of the traditional cuisine of the Tamils, in the last hundred years or so they have adopted and adapted many sweets from other cultures.

Tapioca Kool

Maravalli Kool

400 gm   tapioca, de-veined and cubed
½ cup   coconut milk
1 cup   sugar
1 tsp   salt
¼ tsp   crushed cardamom seeds or powder

METHOD

1. Boil tapioca in a covered pot till soft. Mash it.
2. Add coconut milk, sugar and salt. Stir well. Cook for a further two minutes.
3. Add cardamom seeds or powder and remove from stove. May be served warm or cold.

Aadi Kool

1 cup   rice flour
1¼ l   water
2 tbsp   black gram (urad dal)
2 tbsp   green gram (moong dal)
100 gm   jaggery
Flesh of ¼   coconut, diced
3 cups   coconut milk
½ tsp   salt

METHOD

1. Boil water and add black gram and green gram.
2. When cooked, add jaggery and diced coconut. Lower flame and simmer.
3. In a jug, combine coconut milk, salt and rice flour.

4. Dribble this mixture over a spoon into the pot, stirring constantly to avoid forming lumps.
5. Stir till cooked.
6. Serve hot.

Kesari

1 cup semolina
½ cup ghee
7–10 cashew nuts, cut into quarters
7–10 raisins
2 cups water
1½ cups sugar
¼ tsp ground cardamom
4–5 strands saffron, soaked in 2 tsp water
    (or yellow food colouring)

METHOD

1. Roast semolina in a pan or wok over medium heat, stirring continuously. Do not let it burn. When it turns light golden, transfer it to a bowl and allow to cool.
2. Heat 1 teaspoon ghee in a heavy-based or non-stick pan. Add ground cardamom and saute cashews and raisins.
3. Add water and sugar. Bring to boil.
4. Reduce heat to 'low'. Add semolina slowly, stirring constantly. Add saffron soaked in water.
5. Simmer for 2 minutes until water is absorbed.
6. Add remaining ghee and turn over continuously till the mixture leaves the sides of the pan. Remove from stove.
7. Smooth into a shallow container and cut into squares or diagonals when cool.

Sago Payasam

Saversi Payasam

1 cup sago
1 tsp ghee
100 gm cashew nuts
100 gm sultanas

3 cups water
4 dessertspoons sugar
½ cup milk
Seeds from 3 cardamom pods

METHOD

1. Heat ghee and gently fry cashew nuts and sultanas. Set aside.
2. Cook sago in water till it becomes transparent.
3. Add sugar. Stir well.
4. Add milk. Continue to cook till it boils.
5. Add cardamom seeds, roasted cashews and sultanas.
6. Simmer for a few minutes. Remove and serve warm.

Rice Payasam

Arisi Payasam

1 cup long grained rice
3 cups water
1 cup coconut milk or fresh milk
A pinch of salt
¼ cup roasted split green gram (moong dal)
¼ cup scraped (grated) coconut
1 cup jaggery pieces or brown sugar
2 tbsp ghee
1 tbsp cashew nuts, chopped
1 tbsp raisins
½ tsp ground or crushed cardamom seeds
3–4 strands saffron soaked in 1 tsp warm water (optional)

METHOD

1. Boil together water, coconut milk, rice, salt and green gram. Add 1 tablespoon ghee.
2. When cooked, add scraped (grated) coconut and jaggery.
3. Heat the other tablespoon of ghee, and sauté chopped cashew nuts, raisins, crushed cardamom. Add to the rice payasam.
4. If using it, add saffron water and stir well.
5. Serve warm.

Vermicelli Payasam

Semiya Payasam

½ cup vermicelli
1 tsp ghee
1 cup boiling water
1 cup sugar
½ cup milk
A pinch saffron strands, soaked in a tsp water
5–6 cashew nuts, cut into small pieces
1 dessertspoon sultanas or raisins
½ tsp powdered cardamom
¼ tsp powdered cloves or 3 cloves

METHOD

1. Heat ghee and fry vermicelli till golden.
2. Add boiling water and cook till tender.
3. Add sugar and when dissolved, add milk. Bring to boil.
4. Add saffron soaked in water.
5. Add cashew nuts, raisins, cardamom powder and cloves.
6. Cook through and remove from flame.
7. Serve warm.

Green Gram Payasam

Pasipayaru Payasam

½ cup whole green gram (moong dal), washed well
3 tsp ghee
3 cups boiling water
½ cup sugar
1 cup milk
6 cashew nuts cut into small pieces
½ tsp powdered cardamom
½ tsp powdered cloves
Tiny slices of coconut flesh (optional)

Method

1. Heat 2 teaspoons of ghee in a pan. Fry green gram till it begins to turn brown.
2. Add boiling water and cook till green gram is very soft.
3. Add sugar and when it has dissolved, add the milk.
4. Heat remaining ghee in smaller pan. Fry cashew nuts, powdered cardamom and cloves. Add to payasam.
5. Add slivers of coconut (optional). Cook for a further 2–3 minutes.
6. Remove from stove and serve warm.

Fried String Hoppers in Syrup

Pori Idiappam

2 cups rice flour, roasted
1 cup coconut milk
¼ cup water
½ tsp salt
½ cup sugar
Oil for frying

Method

1. Boil coconut milk, water and salt.
2. Add to rice flour. Mix well.
3. Make string hoppers using a string hopper 'ural'. (For recipe for String Hoppers see p. 2.)
4. Heat oil. Deep-fry string hoppers.
5. Arrange string hoppers in a dish.
6. To make syrup boil sugar in 2 tablespoons of water.
7. Pour sugar syrup over string hoppers.
8. Serve as a sweet dish.

Jaggery Pudding

Pananggatti Pudding

4 tbsp cornflour
4 cups thin coconut milk
1½ cups jaggery pieces

A pinch of salt
1 cup grated coconut, lightly roasted
½ tsp powdered cardamom
1 cup thick coconut milk

METHOD

1. Blend cornflour with a little thin coconut milk.
2. In a saucepan heat remaining thin coconut milk.
3. Add 1 cup jaggery pieces and salt.
4. Add the blended cornflour stirring briskly to prevent lumps from forming. (If lumps form, remove from stove and beat with a rotary beater with a teaspoon of butter to make it smooth again.)
5. Add grated and roasted coconut and cardamom powder.
6. Continue to cook till mixture thickens.
7. Coat a pudding mould with a little milk or coconut milk.
8. Pour mixture into the mould. Allow it to set at room temperature.
9. Dissolve remaining jaggery in thick coconut milk over a very low flame.
10. Cool and serve with pudding.

Purple Yam Pudding

Rasavelli Kalee

500 gm purple yam (rasavelli kilangu), peeled and diced
Enough water to cover yam
½ cup thick coconut milk
½ cup sugar
¼ tsp salt
¼ tsp vanilla essence (optional)

METHOD

1. Wash yam a few times to remove the slimey residue.
2. Put in a pot with enough water to cover yam. Cook till soft.
3. Mash yam very well while in the pot.
4. Add coconut milk, sugar and salt. Mix thoroughly and turn off flame.
5. Add vanilla essence, if desired.
6. Grease a tray with a little ghee. Dish yam on to greased tray. When cool, cut into pieces and serve as a teacake or dessert. If a more liquid porridge-like consistency is required, double the amount of coconut milk and add ½ cup water.

Rock Sugar Kool

Karkandu Kool

¾ cup rock sugar, pounded or ground
½ cup roasted long grained rice flour
3 cups coconut milk
¼ cup roasted green gram (moong dal)
1½ cups water
1½ cups tiny slices of coconut flesh
A pinch of salt

METHOD

1. Mix rice flour in coconut milk.
2. Boil green gram in water.
3. When almost cooked, add rice flour and coconut milk.
4. As mixture thickens add rock sugar, pieces of coconut and salt.
5. Cook till sugar dissolves.
6. Remove and serve warm.

Wood-Apple Cream

Vilaampala Kool

2 cups wood-apple pulp
1 cup thin coconut milk
½ cup thick coconut milk
½ cup palm sugar (jaggery)

METHOD

1. Mix wood-apple pulp in thin coconut milk and stir well.
2. Strain to remove all fibrous parts and seeds.
3. Mix with thick coconut milk and palm jaggery.
4. Serve cold.

Curry Powders

Traditionally curry powders were ground fresh on the 'ammi' or grinding stone, so much so that they were more paste than powders. But for convenience, most cooks combined the dry ingredients and pounded them together. This would be done on the family pounding block. It was far easier, of course, to clean all ingredients and dry or roast them and then take them to the flour mill to get them ground. This powder could then be stored for months.

Basic Curry Powder

500 gm   dried red chillies
    (with stem for hotter, without stem for milder mixtures)
2 cups   coriander seeds
A small piece of turmeric root
¼ cup   black peppercorns
½ cup   cumin seeds

METHOD
1. Wash all ingredients separately.
2. Roast them separately.
3. Mix them together and dry grind them.
4. Store in an airtight container and use as required.

Chilli Powder

500 gm   dried red chillies, stems removed

METHOD
1. Wash and sun-dry the chillies.
2. Dry grind them.
3. Store in an airtight container.

Fish Curry Powder

1 part curry powder
1½   parts chilli powder

METHOD

1. Mix the two powders together throughly.
2. Store in an airtight container.

This may be used for fish preparations.

Charakku Curry Powder

250 grams coriander seeds
3 tsp peppercorns
2 tsp cumin seeds
2 tsp fenugreek seeds
8 tsp fennel seeds
5–7 curry leaves
a tiny piece turmeric root
2 tsp mustard seeds
2 tsp parboiled rice

METHOD

1. Separately wash and sun-dry well coriander, peppercorns, cumin, fenugreek and fennel seeds.
2. Cut the curry leaves fine. Roast together with coriander and turmeric root. Set aside.
3. Roast each spice separately and set aside.
4. Mix all the ingredients together.
5. Dry grind and store in an airtight container.

This may be used wherever chilli is not desired, such as in foods for nursing mothers and invalids.

Glossary

English	Tamil	Hindi

Spices

English	Tamil	Hindi
Asafoetida	Perungaayam	Hing
Cardamom	Elakkai	Elaichi
Cloves	Kirambu	Lavang
Coriander	Malli	Hara dhania
Cumin	Nachjeeragam	Zeera
Curry leaf	Karuvapillai	Kari patta
Fennel seeds	Perumjeeragam	Saunf
Fenugreek seeds	Venthiam	Methi
Mustard seeds	Kadugu	Rai
Pepper	Milagu	Kali mirch
Sesame seeds	Ellu	Til
Tamarind	Puli	Imli
Turmeric	Manjal	Haldi
Oregano	Omam	Ajwain

Vegetables, pulses, lentils

English	Tamil	Hindi
Ash plantain	Vaalakkaai	Kela (hara)
Aubergine/Eggplant (brinjal)	Kaththarikkaai	Baigan
Bengal gram	Kadalai paruppu	Channa dal
Bitter gourd	Pavakkaai	Karela
Black gram	Ulunthu (ulutham paruppu)	Urad dal
Bottle gourd	Churakkaai	Lauki
Drumstick	Murunggakkaai	Sajan ki phalli
Green gram	Pasi payaru	Moong dal
Indian pennywort	Vallaarai keerai	
Long beans	Paithanggaai	
Margossa	Vepam	Neem
Okra	Vendikkaai	Bhindi
Purple yam	Rasavalli kilangu	
Ripe jackfruit	Pilapadzam	Kathal
Snake gourd	Pidalangaai	Chachinda
Sago	Chavvarisi	Sago
Wood apple	Vilaampadzam	Kaith
Young jackfruit	Pilaakkaai	Kathal

Glossary of parts of the Palmyra palm used in cooking

Jaggery: This is a dark brown crumbly sugar made from karupani, the nectar from the flowers of the male tree. The karupani is boiled and the thickened sugar poured into tiny containers woven out of the palmyra leaves. These are called 'karupatti'.

Kalaakaram: As with jaggery, a form of sugar called kalaakaram is made from karupani. This is prized for its medicinal properties.

Karupani: the sweet nectar from the male palmyra palm.

Kilangu: The root of the seedlings of the palmyra. This is either dried to become Odiyal, or it is parboiled and then dried to become Pulukkodiyal. (See below.)

Nongu: the colourless fleshy kernel of the fruit. There are three in each fruit.

Odiyal: The roots are sun-dried to become Odiyal. They can be sliced before drying. These dried roots are frequently packed as a nutritious snack for the traveller, the long-distance pilgrim and the field worker.

Palmyra Fruit Pulp: Choose a ripe palmyra fruit. Peel the skin (often it is thrown into embers to soften it before peeling). Sprinkle the flesh with water to soften it. Scrape off the flesh with a spoon. Strain the flesh through a medium-holed sieve to remove any fibre.

Pulukkodiyal: The seeds of the palmyra fruit are collected and put into nurseries. Here they are watered and tended for almost three-and-a-half months. When thick roots are formed, the seeds are lifted and the roots removed. They are washed, skinned and then parboiled. After they have been sun-dried they become Pulukkodiyal.

Odiyal Flour: This is obtained by grinding the Odiyal root into flour. It is rather bitter and so has to be washed well to eliminate the bitterness. Nevertheless, it is an important ingredient in Tamil cuisine, being rich in fibre and Vitamin B. Hence its usage in Jaffna specialities.

Toddy: When Karupani from the palmyra palm is fermented it becomes the intoxicating toddy. This milky white drink is also used for medicinal and culinary purposes.

Cooking Terms

Bring to boil: To allow the ingredients to boil once, before proceeding to the next step.

Dry grind: Grinding without any liquid, either on the grinding stone or in an electric grinder or food processor.

Pound: Traditionally pounding was done in an 'ural'—a heavy mortar made of the trunk of the jackfruit tree—and a long 'ulakkai'—a heavy round beam about 4–6 inches in diameter. For some dishes the use of a pounding action cannot be replaced by the modern grinders. A large mortar and pestle may be substituted.

Roast: To toss (without oil) over a low flame, in a wok or a heavy-based pan.

Temper: To sauté in very little oil, tempering spices such as mustard seeds, dried chillies (as required by the recipe) to be added to the dish to enhance flavours.

Toss together (as on the stove): Mix by turning over and over again using a flat wooden or metal ladle or spatula.

Thread-like consistency: When a drop of syrup is taken between thumb and index finger and pulled apart, it forms a thread.

English – Index

Tamil – Index